teach yourself®

letter-writing skills

letter-writing skills

david james
revised by
anthony masters

For over 60 years, more than 40 million people have learnt over 750 subjects the **teach yourself** way, with impressive results.

be where you want to be
with **teach yourself**

For UK order queries: please contact Bookpoint Ltd, 130 Milton Park, Abingdon, Oxon OX14 4SB. Telephone: (44) 01235 827720. Fax: (44) 01235 400454. Lines are open from 9.00–18.00, Monday to Saturday, with a 24-hour message answering service. You can also order through our website: www.madaboutbooks.com

For U.S.A order queries: please contact McGraw-Hill Customer Services, P.O. Box 545, Blacklick, OH 43004-0545, U.S.A. Telephone: 1-800-722-4726. Fax: 1-614-755-5645.

For Canada order queries: please contact McGraw-Hill Ryerson Ltd, 300 Water St, Whitby, Ontario L1N 9B6, Canada. Telephone: 905 430 5000. Fax: 905 430 5020.

Long-renowned as the authoritative source for self-guided learning – with more than 30 million copies sold worldwide – the *Teach Yourself* series includes over 300 titles in the fields of languages, crafts, hobbies, business and education.

A catalogue entry for this title is available from The British Library.

Library of Congress Catalog Card Number: 94-68413

First published in UK 1995 by Contemporary Books, A Division of the McGraw Hill Companies, 4255 West Touhy Avenue, Lincolnwood (Chicago), Illinois 60646 – 1975 U.S.A.

This edition published 2003.

Typeset by Transet Limited, Coventry, England.
Printed in Great Britain for Hodder & Stoughton Educational, a division of Hodder Headline Ltd, 338 Euston Road, London NW1 3BH by Cox & Wyman Ltd, Reading, Berkshire.

Impression number 7 6 5 4 3 2
Year 2007 2006 2005 2004 2003

contents

acknowledgements

The publishers gratefully thank the following for permission to reproduce material in this book.

David Higham Associates for the extract from *Selected Letters* by Dylan Thomas, page 17; Faber & Faber for the extract from *Sylvia Plath Letters Home*, page 15; Ann Walden and Helen Gansa. Thanks also to those whose names have been withheld.

Every effort has been made to trace and acknowledge ownership of copyright.

introduction

Although fashion, form and formalities in letter writing change with considerable speed, there are basic rules and methods of approach that should be followed. They apply to writing a letter for a job, a letter to a friend or a letter to the local authority, and it is these rules and methods which form the basis of this book. If they are followed carefully it will be possible for a reader to write satisfactory letters on a great number of subjects, and to a wide range of people.

The general principles of letter writing are outlined in the first pages of this book and advice on basic points is given. They are then applied to the writing of personal and domestic letters and applications for jobs, as well as communications with the authorities, businesses and the media. There is also a chapter on the Internet and e-mail and the text concludes with methods of addressing people and the use of abbreviations.

Having read this book, you should feel more confident about achieving concise, accurate and interesting letters whether you are writing to a friend or the bank manager.

before you start

In this chapter you will learn:

- **about various stationery options available to you – and about getting personalized stationery printed**
- **about the pros and cons of handwriting or typing your letters**
- **how to lay out your letter**
- **the correct way to begin and end a letter**
- **the advantages of making a rough draft before you write or type the final version**
- **which punctuation is best to use, and which is best avoided**
- **about legal implications, such as libel and copyright.**

Whatever kind of letter you are writing, there are important rules to be observed. Whether you are making an application for a job, raising a query about a holiday booking, or writing a protest to the local authority, if these rules are followed you are more likely to achieve the results you are looking for.

You will want your letter to be read easily, and without too much effort by the reader. You will want the letter's contents to be taken seriously and to create an impression that you are a person whose requests, complaints or views cannot be brushed aside.

Thousands of letters are opened every morning, and not all will get as much attention at the receiving end as they may deserve. Those that do are the ones that are well expressed.

Notepaper

You can write on plain notepaper, or use headed. A business should always use headed notepaper and, even for private letters, many people have their address and telephone number printed at the top.

The cost of printing, however, can be expensive, and if you write only a few letters you may not think this worth while. Your address and telephone number can be neatly written or typed at the top.

You should always buy the best quality paper that you can afford. White or cream is the most distinctive.

Paper sizes – of which the most familiar were quarto (8in × 11in) and foolscap (8in × 13in) – have given way to new sizes. These have been worked out on a complicated system – based on a rectangle having an area of one square metre. There are eleven sizes, all prefixed with the letter 'A', and the sizes most likely to concern the average letter-writer are A4, which is 210mm by 297mm (8.27in × 11.69in); A5, which is 148mm by 210mm (5.83in × 8.27in) and A6, which is 105mm by 148mm (4.13in × 5.83in). Whether you are concerned primarily with private stationery or with business stationery (nowadays the A4 size) there is much to be said for choosing a simple typeface for your address.

Even the smallest jobbing printer can give good advice here. For instance, white paper and black print is clear and makes a good impression on the recipient.

In some businesses – ranging from a design group to a florist – colour can be an advantage and a logo is often incorporated in the address. The basic rule is to use notepaper that expresses your personality, or that of your business, and will be treated with respect.

As far as envelopes are concerned, make sure that they not only match your paper in tone and quality, but that your letters will fit into them neatly.

Handwritten and typewritten/ wordprocessed letters

Next comes the choice of typing or writing your letter, a choice not as clear cut as it was when all business letters were typed and most private letters were written by hand. In fact, it was once considered extremely 'bad form' to type private letters. With the spread of computers this inhibition has faded, although there are still some occasions where the use of a computer would give the wrong impression. Letters of condolence are a good example of this, as would be a letter to an old friend. It is always a good idea to hand write any letter which you hope will convey a personal sincerity to the recipient. On the other hand, a handwritten business letter can – unless it is very neatly written – arouse only irritation in a busy office.

If you are writing by hand and your recipient is not a long-suffering but tolerant friend, you must ensure your letter is easily readable. This can be achieved by following a few simple rules, the first of which is that the letters forming the words should be neither too big nor too small.

A well-known scientist who died some years ago wrote in letters only a sixteenth of an inch high and with strokes 'above' and 'below' the line hardly any bigger; only one member of his staff was able to read the important letters which he wrote in this minuscule script.

By contrast, a famous British politician wrote in such large script that even a few short words stretched across the full width of the page. To achieve a happy medium, the words should be separated by gaps of the same width, since this makes any page far easier to read. The lines of writing should be as horizontal as possible. The real aim when writing a letter is that it should be read, not that it should demonstrate the character of the writer.

All this helps to emphasize the obvious advantage that typing or e-mail has over handwriting; it can be read with only minimal difficulty compared with the problem of deciphering script that is not always legible.

If you write your letters instead of typing them, and unless your signature is impeccably legible, make sure you print your name in brackets underneath your signature. This can be a great relief to a reader when he finds that he does not have to decide whether the letter he has read came from 'Clark', 'Stark', 'Cleach' or 'Plant'.

Laying out your letter

If the paper has no printed heading, your telephone number should be written in the top right-hand corner. Slightly below this goes the date on which you are writing. Opposite, on the left (or on the left at the bottom of the page, level with your signature) goes the name and address of the person to whom you are writing; this is necessary with business letters, but not with private letters.

10 Osprey Street
Sunningham
Loamshire
[Post/Zip Code]

Mr James Bennet
Secretary
Forest Tennis Club
32 Burton Avenue
Sunningham
[Post/Zip Code]

January 2nd, 2003

Dear Mr Bennet,
My wife and I have only recently moved to Sunningham. When we lived in Hopton we enjoyed playing tennis at our local club, and I would be most grateful if you could let me have membership details for the Forest Tennis Club.

Yours sincerely,
James Cartwright

When writing a business letter it is sometimes useful to put a brief, underlined heading as an indication of what the letter is about just below the 'Dear Mr Brown'. It might be, for instance, <u>Claim for cancelled hotel booking</u> or <u>Re: Proposed</u>

Ending of Burtonshire Bus Company Route No 45. If you are replying to a business letter, this may have a reference number, in which case you can put this in place of the identifying words above – i.e. Your Ref. No. 123. This should at least prevent your letter from floating round various uninterested departments before finding its way to the right desk.

There is now the layout itself to be considered, and this will depend on the length of your letter. It will look at its best if it is well spaced on the page, with rather more white space below the end of it than there is at the top, and with good margins at the sides. Two problems should be avoided. The first is writing a short letter with the lines close together, so that the final product has an immense area of white space filling the bottom two-thirds of the paper. The second is bringing the end of your letter so close to the bottom of the paper that there is hardly any room left for the conclusion and signature. The first mistake can be avoided by double- or even treble-spacing the letter if you are typing, or by giving the lines an equal amount of 'air' if you are writing by hand. In the second case just leave an inch or two of white at the foot of the page and continue on the other side.

Starting and finishing

Starting and ending a private letter is more straightforward than starting and ending a business letter. In writing to a neighbour, depending on the relationship, you should either address him as 'Dear Mr Smith', 'Dear John Smith' or 'Dear John' and conclude 'Yours sincerely'.

In business letters there is more scope for variety and mistakes. During the last quarter-century business letters have become far less formal than they once were. There is rarely need to go to the lengths of what was common before the Second World War, when 'Sir' or 'Madam', written on a single line, was the customary way of starting a letter to strangers.

'Dear Mr Montgomery' is the safest way to begin a letter to someone you have never met, unless, of course, he has one of the ranks or titles which are dealt with in Chapter 7. In all cases a writer who does not trouble to find out the sex of the person to whom he is writing will not get, or deserve, much attention. 'Dear Mrs Cunningham' is the right way to address a woman. Ending a letter 'Yours sincerely' is an easy and safe way to conclude a letter. Try not to use 'Dear Sir/Madam', but if this is unavoidable, you should end the letter with 'Yours faithfully'.

Drafting a letter

Whether you are writing a letter of condolence to a friend or a letter of complaint to your Member of Parliament, it is important to start with a rough draft of what you want to say. This will make for a more concise and effective end result. For some of us letter writing comes easily, but although words may flow when writing to a friend, stating a case or making a forceful complaint needs careful thought and exact expression.

First work out precisely what you want to say, the points you need to make, and the most telling way of putting them across. Always remember that it is vital to have these points clear in your mind before you even begin the rough drafting. A mind churning with words and phrases, but without any firm ideas to harness them to, will get you nowhere.

When preparing to write a letter, decide what the main point is. This should come first, followed by the 'evidence', or similar material, and then a brief conclusion. If you think the result sounds too abrupt and clinical, remember that a good letter-writer could well follow the advice given to a public speaker: 'Stand up, speak up, and shut up.' In other words, say what is essential, but no more.

Making a rough draft will also enable you to weed out from your letter certain phrases that are natural and acceptable when spoken but which can be damaging if they appear in a formal letter. When you read over your draft before writing or typing the final version, make sure you remove those phrases. Even the most experienced writer can fall into the trap of letting these slip into a rough draft so do not worry about that. You are in good company!

Be careful about phrases like 'OK', 'haven't a clue', 'couldn't care less' and 'puts you off'. Cut out all the slang expressions and colloquialisms which you might normally use in casual conversation. They can make easy reading in a newspaper or magazine article, where they are quite appropriate, but are out of place in a formal letter. Furthermore, they are a sign of the inexperienced letter-writer, and that is not the impression you want to create.

Not all of this applies, of course, to letters to friends and acquaintances. There you can be as free and easy as you wish. The secret of intimate personal letter writing is spontaneity, as if you are talking to the person who is reading the letter.

But in the case of making a complaint to a shopkeeper you know, it is important to be businesslike without sounding so formal that you stand in danger of spoiling a good relationship. In other words, state your grievance clearly and concisely, but keep the tone of your letter friendly.

When writing formal letters, slang and colloquialisms must be avoided, but so must phrases that go to the other extreme and which are left over from a business age that is long dead.

You should not write of 'your letter of the 10th inst.', but 'your letter dated the 10th of this month'. One should not 'beg for the favour of an early reply', but ask 'for a reply as soon as possible'. 'I am desirous of' is only a more pompous way of saying 'I wish to'. Avoid saying 'This is OK by us', but also avoid saying that you 'find the aforementioned entirely in accordance with our views'. It will be better if you just say 'I approve of your idea'. People 'die' rather than 'pass away', and it is better to say that you 'do not think' rather than that you 'are not of the opinion'. Another horror is 're' when what you really mean is 'about'.

There are also some words which are quite suitable in one context and utterly unsuitable in another. For instance, it is correct to write of 'per cent' or 'per capita', but wrong to write 'as per my letter' when what you really mean is 'as I said in my letter'. The rule should always be to use short, simple phrases which are quite clear, rather than those which are complicated and ambiguous: in other words, 'wash basins' rather than 'ablution facilities'.

These are examples of the stilted English which tries to give an air of importance to a simple statement and should be avoided at all costs. The rule of thumb is to use the plain, straightforward expression, the precise word in an economical sentence, so ask yourself whether you have said what you wanted to say exactly and simply. You can get a lot of help in this very essential process from *A Dictionary of Modern English Usage* by H.W. Fowler, published by the Oxford University Press.

Punctuation

This is used to make the writer's meaning clear and whether you are writing a love letter, a complaint to a business, or an application for a job, making yourself clear is essential.

Every sentence requires a full stop at the end to show that it is completed, and long sentences may require one or more commas, a semi-colon or even a colon. Commas should not be scattered about; instead, each should indicate there is a pause in the sentence. In other words, there would be a physical pause to help make the meaning clear if the sentence were being read aloud. There should be a mental pause if the sentence is being read to oneself.

The purpose of the comma in bringing about a pause is the reason behind most of the 'rules' which have grown up about its usage. One of these rules is that when an adjective is immediately followed by one or more adjectives, a comma is always placed after each except the last. For example: 'I am selling a good car', 'I am selling a good, economical car', 'I am selling a good, economical, trustworthy car'. But if the succession of adjectives is interrupted by 'and', then this itself has the effect of creating a pause and you would write: 'This is a good, economical and trustworthy car'.

Sometimes the use or non-use of a comma can affect the actual meaning of a sentence. If, for instance, you write: 'I am returning your cheque, which lacks a signature' you are really saying: 'I am returning your cheque. It lacks a signature.' If, however, you leave out the comma and write: 'I am returning your cheque which lacks a signature', this means that you are returning one out of many cheques received, i.e. the one which lacks a signature.

It should always be possible to remove the words between two commas and yet leave the sentence making grammatical sense. Therefore, it would be wrong to write: 'I told the chairman that, we all sympathized with his dilemma, but we could not support his action.' If the commas were removed the sentence would be grammatically correct but no special emphasis would be given to the fact 'that we all sympathized'. The problem is solved as follows: 'I told the chairman that, while we all sympathized with his dilemma, we could not support his action.'

In some cases the job done by commas can be carried out by brackets or by two dashes. These devices were more popular years ago, when sentences in most business letters, as well as some private letters, tended to be longer than they are today. A long sentence spattered with commas can be confusing, however well they are used, and it was quite common to see such sentences as 'Mr Jones (who was not very co-operative at our last meeting) seemed most anxious to help, although it is still apparent, I am afraid, that he is not very much in favour of the scheme – if, in fact, he is in favour of it at all – and that we may well face opposition in the future.'

Nowadays, shorter sentences are less confusing, and the use of both brackets and dashes has declined. Do not use either unless you feel that it is really necessary.

Other forms of punctuation are the semi-colon and the colon. The semi-colon is used to break up a long sentence into more easily understood parts. The head of a firm might write, 'We are going to give the staff an outing; we are going to take them down to the coast for the day; and if the idea is a success we are going to repeat it next year.' The colon is used when you have to make a statement and then follow it up with an explanation. For example, 'There were six of us present: John, Jack, James, Mary, Maria and Miranda.'

If the colon is used before a number of words, phrases or even paragraphs, it shows that all these are governed by the preceding sentence, which does not have to be repeated. This is a way of setting it out:

Would you please note the following points:

1 Whatever dates are arranged, it is vital we are back in London by the end of May.
2 The total cost of the trip must not exceed £X.
3 Train travel must be kept to a minimum.

A punctuation mark to avoid is the exclamation mark, particularly in business letters. In private correspondence it does not matter so much, but it should still be used with care. If you feel that an exclamation mark is necessary and that the sentence is not sufficiently emphatic without it, try re-wording the sentence. There is no rule against writing: 'You have done this entirely without my permission!!' but it is better to re-word the sentence as follows: 'I want to protest strongly against this having been done without my permission.'

Another form of punctuation where caution should be taken is the inverted comma or quotation mark (either single or double), which is always used in pairs. There are three general uses for quotation marks:

1. To show the words between them are not the writer's own, but someone else's, and at the same time to emphasize their importance. Take the sentence: 'Smith says that he will not attend any more meetings, whatever the reason for their being called.' It would be more telling to write: 'Smith says that he "will not attend any more meetings, whatever the reason for their being called".' The device must only be used when there is some obvious point to it; there would be little point in writing 'Smith says he "has received your letter".' In fact to write the sentence that way would be to imply that while Smith had in fact received your letter there was doubt as to whether he was going to do anything about it. If quoting from a report, too many quotation marks may appear irritating. A better plan would be to enclose with the letter a copy of the report, with certain passages marked.
2. Another use of inverted commas is to show that a word or phrase is not used in its normal literal meaning. Thus you might write: 'What I am most concerned about is the "atmosphere" of the meeting.'
3. The third use involves enclosing in inverted commas a phrase that is not normally used in a letter. You might write: 'If we did this the younger members of the group would probably think that we were not "with it".'

Legal implications

It is essential to consider whether the letter you have written has any legal implications.

Firstly, you should, of course, take care not to commit yourself in writing to anything you are not prepared to buy or to do, and you shouldn't sign an agreement or a contract without having given it very careful thought.

Secondly, there is the important question of libel. The difference between slander and libel is that the first is spoken and the second written. However, they both have one thing in common: they bring someone into 'hatred, ridicule or contempt'.

The law of defamation, which includes both slander and libel, is extremely complicated and it is almost impossible to state whether certain written words and phrases are defamatory until the Court decides the issue. Anyone writing a letter containing words which could conceivably be construed as bringing someone into 'hatred, ridicule or contempt' should definitely leave them out.

It is no defence to say that you did not intend to libel. Provision is made in the libel laws for what is known as fair comment on a matter of public interest. However, this can be interpreted in various ways and your understanding of this may differ from that of the Court!

Put yourself in the position of the person you are writing to – or of anyone else mentioned in the letter. Then ask yourself whether, if you received the letter yourself, you might feel your reputation or that of anyone else had been diminished. If there is the slightest doubt, think again.

Thirdly, a point that is more likely to affect letters you receive than letters you write, is the matter of copyright. In written material this belongs to the person who wrote the letter and *not* to the person who receives and legally owns it. There are some qualifications to this. If, for instance, you write a letter to a newspaper, it is obvious that you want the paper to publish it. Although the copyright is yours you have given the paper the right to print it on this occasion. Where problems may arise is in the case of letters written between neighbours or acquaintances.

At some future date Ms Jones, who has received a letter from Ms Smith, may wish to publish it. But although she physically and legally owns the letter, the copyright in its contents belongs to Ms Smith and if Ms Jones wishes to use it she should ask the permission of Ms Smith before doing so.

The point to be made here is that if you have a letter which you believe supports your case in an argument you should consider the position carefully before using it. Minor infringements of copyright, however, are unlikely to be taken very seriously, but there are always the exceptions. Unfortunately, ignorance of the law is no excuse.

Before you post your letter ask yourself one last question: have I made any promise, legally binding or otherwise, which will cause me worry, expense or embarrassment if I have to fulfil it. This illustrates a more general rule. Draft your letters one day, 'sleep on them', then read the drafts again, even more carefully, before putting them in the post.

Finally, make sure that you enclose with the letter any documents which you have said you are enclosing. They are required when writing for a car licence, or insurance, or when writing for information from some organization which has asked for a SAE (stamped addressed envelope) before you get a reply. Check that you have enclosed what was required.

the art of personal letter writing

In this chapter you will learn:

- about different types of letters, including letters of condolence, congratulation, thanks, complaint
- about the often sensitive issue of letters to neighbours
- about letters you may be asked to write as a reference for someone you know
- about letters concerning groups or societies
- about letters concerned with booking a holiday
- about personal letter writing.

Personal letter writing has been heavily eroded by other forms of communication, but it still remains the most intimate and can be far more reflective than any other. A telephone call, although it provides spontaneity, does not give the same opportunity for considered thought.

In a letter one can really be oneself and much more accurately and instinctively reflect personal feelings. The American poet, Sylvia Plath, wrote hundreds of deeply expressive letters to her mother. This one, written on 13 October, 1954, is a typical example:

Dearest Mother,

... Now I think it is the time for me to concentrate on the hard year ahead, and I do so, although it means sacrificing the hours spent in pleasant frivolity over coffee and bridge – but I feel that the work I'm doing now is most important for the last push of my senior year – and I know how to have happy gay times when I really want to.

... I know that underneath the blazing jaunts in yellow convertibles to exquisite restaurants I am really regrettably unoriginal, conventional, and puritanical basically, but I needed to practise a certain healthy bohemianism for a while to wring away from the gray-clad, basically-dressed, brown-haired, clock-regulated, responsible, salad-eating, water-drinking, bed-going, economical, practical girl that I had become – and that's why I needed to associate with people who were very different from myself. My happiest times were those entertaining in the apartment [the preceding summer, at Cambridge, Mass., while attending Harvard summer school], where I could merrily create casseroles and conversation for small intimate groups of people I like very much and that served as a balance in the midst of the two extremes.

... I am a firm believer in learning to be inventive and independent the hard way – with little or no money, and I hope I can continue to investigate life's chances and try to be so even though inside I long for comforting security and someone to blow my nose for me, just the way most people do. I was proud of learning to cook and take care of bills this summer, but that is only the beginning. If only England would by some miracle come through, I would be forced shivering into a new, unfamiliar world, where I had to forge anew friends and a home

for myself, and although such experiences are painful and awkward at first, I know, intellectually, that they are the best things to make one grow – always biting off just a slight bit more than you chewed before and finding to your amazement that you can, when it comes right down to it, chew that too!

... Right now it seems as if it is impossible that I [will] ever have a well-written thesis done, because now all reading is apparently unrelated (except that it is all about doubles and very exciting in itself) and thoughts are yet in embryo. The rough draft of my first chapter is due in a week from this Friday, and I am wondering if I can say anything original or potential in it, as I feel always that I have not enough incisive thinking ability – the best thing is that the topic itself intrigues me and that no matter how I work on it, I shall never tire of it. It is specific, detailed, and with a wealth of material; but, of course, I don't know yet what precise angle I'll handle it from. I'm taking the double in Dostoevsky's second novelette, The Double, and Ivan Karamazov (with his Smerdyakov and Devil) in "The Brothers" as cases in point and I think I shall categorize the type of "double" minutely, contrasting and comparing the literary treatment as it corresponds to the intention of psychological presentation. In conjunction with this, I've been reading stories all about doubles, twins, mirror images, and shadow reflections. Your book gift, The Golden Bough, comes in handy, as it has an excellent chapter on "the soul as shadow and reflection".

... Do write often and give my love to all.

Your own sivvy

Dylan Thomas, a past master of begging letters, wrote this to his agent, David Higham, on 20 February, 1939:

Dear Higham,

I'm sorry to be so long returning these stories and suggesting, for Dent's, the ones which I should like to be included in my book of verse and prose. But I've been trying hard to raise enough money to keep my wife and son going for the next month or two, and unsuccessfully. Now I'm relying entirely on Dent's. They've got the ms of the poems, and here are the stories. Of the stories I suggest The Orchards, The Enemies, The Map of Love, A Prospect of the Sea, and The

Visitor. Those are all stories to which no objection, other than literary, could be taken, and anyway they're the best – especially in a book also to contain poems. Church has, among the ms of the poems, part of a prose-piece called 'In the Direction of the Beginning' – a title I originally intended as the title of the whole of the book. I have, however, been considering this piece, and have now decided to make it part of a much longer work which I want to spread over many months to come. But that decision doesn't alter the book: there are still sixteen poems and five stories; and two poems, now finished but not polished up enough yet, to be added. So that Dent's have the whole ms of the whole book, only not yet finally arranged in order – surely a small consideration considering that the book will not be published until after the spring. (Church can, of course, choose other stories from the enclosed collection if he wants to, but I'm sure my choice is right for the purpose of this book.) And, having the ms in their hands, can't they be persuaded to give me the £30 promised on 'Completion of ms'? If they can't be persuaded, then I'm sunk. And this is no begging or joke. I can't return with my family to Wales until some important debts there, principally for rent, have been settled; and there's no money, other than Dent's promised money, coming to me in the world. Do please do your very best for me. After all, here is the book they wanted. The John portrait they can photograph any time they want to – I have all his permission. (By the way, have you heard if they'll do it in colour or not?) And the only thing left to do is to arrange the order of contents. I have, I know, altered the original idea of the book by wishing to cut out the prose-piece already in Church's possession, but I must do that, and five stories and eighteen poems – the two extra ones will be ready and typed by the end of the week – is quite as big a book as Church said he wanted. Please, Higham, do try and get that advance immediately. We've got to move, and we can't until our Welsh village has been pacified financially. I can rely on you, I know, to do your best for me as quickly as you can.

Yours,
Dylan

Most of us write more personal letters than any other sort, and generally they do not pose the above problems. However, there are some letters in this area which do need thinking about, such as letters of condolence, congratulation on birth, engagement or marriage.

Letters of condolence

Letters of condolence can be particularly difficult. You will want to express your feelings of sympathy in the sincerest possible way, but in spite of this there is always an undercurrent of feeling telling you that nothing you can say will help. Nevertheless, knowing that someone is sympathetic can make the recipient deeply moved. Make your letter brief but heartfelt.

There are a few brief rules which can be followed. These are, for instance, one of the few groups of letters which should be written rather than typed. Secondly, no other subject should be mentioned in the letter. Even if there are pressing matters which you want to discuss with the person you are writing to, they should be put in a separate letter and posted on another day.

If you have received the news from a newspaper obituary column, you may have found at the end of it the words: 'No letters'. This means that the relative involved just feels that he or she is incapable of replying adequately.

One of the most important points is to strike the correct balance between writing too much and writing too little. Another is to convey to the recipient the real sympathy you are feeling. The best way of doing this is to use the language of everyday life rather than the words which you may feel are 'proper' in such circumstances. Rigorously avoid writing about the 'sad occasion' or the 'happy release'.

As a warning, consider the letter which you should *not* write. It would go something like this – and, unfortunately, often does:

Dear Jean,

I was honestly shocked to hear from Mrs Jones that your beloved sister had passed away. Patricia had been known to me for many many years and I am sure that she will have told you of all the good times we have together. I know that there is nothing that I can do to help you in the appalling situation with which you are faced, but I nevertheless felt that I should put my condolences on record.

This example includes a number of unsuitable phrases. To start with, 'honestly', which comes out very naturally in conversation, has a slightly different effect when on paper. After all, it should be taken for granted that all the feelings you express are honest; to stress it raises a subconscious suspicion. There should be no need to explain where you got the news from. Mrs Jones may be a mutual acquaintance, but there is no need to drag in a third person.

Brevity is essential. The writer should take it for granted either that the sister was 'beloved' or that Jean would not wish to admit the reverse. 'Passed away' is a relic of an age in which a 'leg' was called a 'limb' and in which a pregnant woman was 'in an interesting condition'. It might be relevant to mention that you had known the sister for some while, but if this is common knowledge in the family, a less heavy-handed reference is all that is needed. If there is nothing you can do to help, don't rub it in. 'Condolences' is far too formal, while putting them 'on record' does suggest that you are only writing because you feel that it is the proper thing to do.

What is called for is something briefer, such as:

Dear Jean,

I was shocked to hear of the death of Patricia, who had been a good friend of mine for many years. Do please accept my sympathy in your loss. If there is anything at all which I can do to help, I do hope that you will ask me.

In addition to the condolence to personal friends, there are those to people not in your immediate circle, such as your doctor, your bank manager or perhaps a neighbour who you barely knew. The letter should be briefer than that to a personal friend:

Dear Mr Arkwright,

I have just learned of the death of your wife. I am so very sorry, and I want to offer my sincere sympathy in your loss.

Letters of congratulation

To congratulate friends on the birth of a child is a happier event, but the letter should still be confined to the one subject. Something like this would be suitable:

Dear Harry and Lorna,

I was delighted to see from the announcement in the local paper today that you have become happy parents.

Congratulations.

Now you can add any question you might have and end the letter simply: 'With all the best of wishes for his (her) – and your – future.'

In sending congratulations on an engagement or a marriage or a partnership, a good deal will depend on how well both parties are known to the letter-writer. To the person you know, you could write like this:

Dear Pamela,

I was so pleased to read of your engagement and am looking forward to meeting your fiancé soon. When will you be married?

Love from Jane.

A similar letter could be sent to the prospective bridegroom if he is the one you know, while if you know both members of the engaged couple, the note should go as follows:

Dear George,

I was happy to see the announcement that you have become engaged to Peggy Gray. I have known you both for a good many years now and can think of no greater happiness for either of you. Do let me know when the day is to be. And once again, congratulations.

If a colleague with whom you are only in touch by letter has passed a professional examination, or if his son or daughter has made a good start on a career, you might want to send a friendly, brief and informal note.

Dear George,

So glad to hear that you passed the Institute's Finals with flying colours. I saw your name on the list in the press and felt that I had to drop you this note, brief as it is.

With all good wishes,
Yours sincerely,

That should be the tone, rather than:

Dear George,

So I see that you are successfully through the Finals. Congratulations! I thought you would do it, but one never knows with examinations.

This sounds too unsupportive.

So, too, with congratulations to a youngster on passing examinations or getting a first job.

Dear Jamie,

I hear from your father that you're starting as a Research Assistant at the new laboratory next month. I know that this is what you've always wanted, so congratulations, and the best of luck for promotion in the future.

You may feel inclined to add advice about working hard, but this would be highly patronizing.

Apart from the letters of congratulation sent to friends or their relatives, there is another large group which does not fall into the category of 'business', even though business acquaintances are involved.

If an acquaintance has been appointed to the Board, promoted to Headmaster, or has made some similar move up the ladder, your exact response will of course depend on how well you know the person concerned. But in most cases you should add your congratulations to a letter dealing with other, routine, matters; and if the letter is typed a PS written in your own hand can do the job effectively. Nothing too formal is needed. 'Sincere congratulations on a well-merited honour' is enough; and, if the recipient is well known to you, the 'step up the ladder' phrase can be used. But unless you are writing to a very old friend, avoid flippancy: 'I never thought the time would come when we would have to call you "Sir"' may be no less than the truth, but it can easily be taken the wrong way.

Whether to write or not depends very largely on two factors: how well you know the person concerned, and how important the honour, appointment, or move up really is. The more important the honour, the less well you need know the recipient before you can write without seeming presumptuous.

Letters of thanks

If a business colleague has done you a favour such as arranging an introduction, or perhaps recommending that you should be given access to a normally 'closed' institution's library, then a brief thank you letter is definitely called for.

Your thank you note need only be very brief along lines such as these:

Dear Mrs Bennet,

I am extremely grateful for your help in obtaining permission for me to use the Sunningham Library. Thank you very much indeed.

Yours sincerely,

In social circles, the thank you letter is still an agreeable courtesy if you have enjoyed a party or a meal. A brief appreciative note is important.

Dear Jane,

Thank you very much for the lovely party on Tuesday. We enjoyed it so much and the dinner was delicious. As always, it was a pleasure to see you all again.

With best wishes,

Sincerely,

Thank you letters provide a valuable opportunity for teaching children how to write. They should be encouraged to write a brief note of thanks for birthday presents. Just a sentence or two is enough, but these should be as legible as the child can make them without getting bored in the process. Of course the very young child will print his or her words, which is a laborious business and a simple: 'Thank you for the present, I loved it' is enough.

Letters to neighbours

This is one of the most difficult areas as care, tact and the exercise of as much restraint as possible is important. Whatever the subject, the chances are that you will have to see – if not talk to – a neighbour for some considerable time, so that even if your letter involves a complaint, try to resolve matters with as little hard feeling as possible. If you should find that you are in the wrong, admit it, however hard the task is.

A letter to someone whom you do not know personally may be written for any one of numerous reasons. If mutual interest is the case the following could apply:

Dear Mrs James,

I have heard from our mutual acquaintance, Mr Westerby, that you are interested in amateur dramatics and I'm wondering whether you would care to join our small group, the Calshot Players, of which I am secretary.

We try to arrange local productions every six months and, apart from this, meet every month to discuss events in the theatre. If you are interested perhaps you would like to come here one evening when I could give you further details of who we are and what we do. Don't worry if you are too busy to contact me. I'll quite understand.

With best wishes,

Yours sincerely,

You may, alternatively, have heard that a new neighbour comes from your own home-town and that you have some mutual acquaintances. In all these cases there are certain guidelines that should be followed. First of all – and unless you really *are* certain of the circumstances – be sure to make the point about 'believing' or 'hearing' of the connection. There is no need to start off on the wrong foot with new neighbours by assuming they come from Yorkshire if in fact they come from Lancashire. Secondly, use your discretion about such phrases as 'heard from Mr Smith'. If Mr Smith has suggested that you get in touch with your new neighbours, all well and good. If not, and if the news of your letter gets back to him, he might well feel that you were just making use of passing gossip and dragging in his name unnecessarily. Finally, remember that even if the neighbours across the road did once have your interests, or the same home-town or some other mutual background, they may not want to renew them. Always include a 'get out' clause and give your correspondent the chance of turning down your proposal without feeling churlish.

A good way to end your letter would be something like this:

> *I do realize that I am taking a liberty in writing to you like this, and if you are not interested I hope you will excuse me. But in any case please accept from me a welcome to the area.*
>
> *Yours sincerely,*

Letters of complaint

Writing to neighbours who have similar interests is one of the more pleasant forms of letter writing. But there are other less agreeable occasions when a letter of complaint is called for. This happens most frequently in urban areas where families live in close proximity to each other and friction can arise without deliberate intention.

Before you start writing a letter of complaint to a neighbour it's a good idea to remember there are two sides to every story; that most local troubles are better resolved by compromise and some measure of goodwill on both sides; and that although the temptation is often to 'go to law', this should be avoided except as a last resort.

The most frequent problem is noise, sometimes a persistently over-loud radio, sometimes the shouts and screams of children or dogs eternally barking. Protests *can* be successful, but they should be embarked on only after less heavy-handed attempts have failed. A start could be made with a letter along these lines:

Dear Mr Jones,

I wonder if you could help my wife and me on something that has been troubling us increasingly during the last weeks. We like to spend most of our evenings quietly and must reluctantly complain about the noise from your radio which we usually hear, more loudly than you may realize, from about 7 o'clock until well after midnight.

I wonder if you would be good enough to tone it down, particularly after 10 o'clock. We would both be grateful if you could help us as we are now regularly losing sleep.

Yours sincerely,

It would be possible to add a further line or two about the nuisance to other neighbours, but that would mean dragging in other people without their consent. You could, of course, refer to any noise-nuisance regulations which might be operating in your area, but to bring up either of these two points at this stage could well act as an irritant.

In most cases the answer to your letter will be co-operative, but if not you must take the next step and send something along these lines:

Dear Mr Jones,

Thank you for your letter of the 7th. I am sorry that you appear unprepared to make your radio less of a persistent nuisance to us. I find that a number of residents in the street are equally unhappy about the noise. I am hoping, therefore, that you will reconsider the situation as we want to avoid taking further action.

Yours sincerely,

The last line may appear to be a little obvious. Naturally everyone wants to avoid taking further action, whether the complaint is a formal one to the local authorities or a request to a solicitor to send a warning letter to the noisy neighbour. Nevertheless the neighbour can be carefully warned at this stage that further action is possible.

'Carefully' is the operative word. To threaten is never good policy, unless you have already thought out how to implement it. If you haven't, you may find yourself in a humiliating position.

If this second step fails, the next possibility is an approach to the relevant environmental department. It is their responsibility to investigate noise pollution and they may well be able to provide a solution which will remove the need for litigation.

You may of course be the subject of a letter of complaint. If so, think carefully before writing a reply. The immediate reaction of most of us when anyone complains about what we are doing is to defend ourselves strongly. But this is a time to be wary. Don't allow emotion to run away with you.

Your first job is to decide whether the complaint is justified or not. We all make mistakes and we are all thoughtless at times, and if you have been annoying your neighbours without realising it, the best thing is to admit it. Honest apologies never do any harm, so your reply should go something like this:

Dear Mrs Turner,

Thank you for your letter of the 17th drawing attention to the way in which our TV annoys you. I never appreciated that the sound penetrated the walls so easily. I apologize for the inconvenience to which you have been put, and will certainly see that the volume is reduced in future. It is also possible that we can help matters by putting the set in a different part of the room. If the noise still continues to trouble you, please let me know and I will see what more can be done.

Yours sincerely,

Let's hope Mrs Turner doesn't have to write again!

Letters concerning groups and societies

If you are thinking of starting a group, a letter to the local paper is often useful.

Dear Editor,

A number of acquaintances have recently suggested that it might be possible to start a local Rambling Club in Torbay. The intention would be to hold a meeting once a month, each member taking it in turn to organize a walk which would start within an hour's drive from Torbay.

In view of the very different rambles which could be planned within a radius of 40 miles, there would seem to be excellent scope for such a club. I would be grateful if anyone interested would get in touch with me at the above address.

Yours faithfully,

Once the scheme gets under way, it will be someone's job to send out the circular letters announcing the monthly meetings and to prepare the annual – or perhaps six-monthly – report of the club's activities. The first can be brief and simple, containing only the necessary facts:

Dear Member,

The club's March walk will be held on the 26th. It will be led by Jack Jones and will start at 10.00 a.m. in the Storrington Market Place.

We could walk for about 12 miles and take a midday break at 'The Hare and Hounds' in Westchester, ending up at Eastern Cross (teas available). The 6.40 p.m. bus from Eastern Cross arrives back in Storrington at 7.15 p.m. Anyone who wants tea should contact Jack Jones by March 19th please.

Yours sincerely,

Rules for the annual report are roughly the same. First, be clear; secondly, be concise, but remember to put at the top of the report exactly what it is:

Report of the Torbay Rambling Club
for the six months ended December 31st, 1997

After that should come a brief summary:

During the six months ended December 31st, 1997, the club held seven meetings. Attendances varied from 25 in June to only 10 in November. A record might have been established at the Christmas meeting on December 28th when 24 members attended. The longest walk was in July when 26 miles were covered, the shortest in October was a circuit of only 10 miles.

After that, you can continue with as much detail as you want, taking care to avoid jokes about those who failed to complete the course, or remained too long over the lunch-time pint.

One task that often falls to the writer of reports is inviting a lecturer or speaker to talk to the club – or, in the case of musical or similar clubs, of inviting an artist to perform. In virtually all cases you need to make enquiries about one point: does the lecturer/speaker normally get paid, or is he/she an enthusiast who requires no fee?

If you can discover only that the lecturer normally asks for a fee but are unable to find out what this is, there is no harm in asking:

Dear Professor,

I am arranging the winter programme of lectures for the Torbay Rambling Club. I would be grateful to know what your fee would be for giving us a talk for an hour or so at some convenient date between September and March. You would of course be our guest at dinner and we would be happy to reimburse your travel expenses.

Our meetings are held in the Clarendon Hall, High Street, Sandyville, and attendances vary between 40 and 80. The hall has excellent facilities for the showing of colour slides and we would of course be delighted if you could illustrate your talk.

Yours,

If the fee is too much, try this:

Dear Professor,

Thank you for your letter of November 5th. I am afraid that the fee you ask is more than a small club such as ours can afford.

However, I know that our members would be extremely interested in your experiences; can we come to a compromise?

Yours sincerely,

A response along these lines will sometimes bring about a reduction in the fee.

When an invitation to talk has been accepted, a further letter will be required. Depending on the circumstances it should incorporate some or all of these points:

Dear Professor,

Thank you very much for agreeing to talk to the Torbay Rambling Club at 8.00 p.m. on February 3rd on your Calais to Rome walk. We have booked a room with bath at the Tor Hotel for the night of the 3rd and I will meet you there at 3.00 p.m. if you are driving down from London. If you are coming by train, I will meet you at the station. The most convenient train is the noon from Paddington which arrives at Tor Cross Station at 5.20 p.m.

If you have any special points to raise please do not hesitate to telephone me at the above number.

Yours sincerely,

One point that can arise when running a local society is that of copyright. You may wish to print on a programme, in an advertisement, or even in an annual report, a quotation from a published book or article.

The copyright in this material will normally be held by the publisher and you must get permission if you want to print a substantial part. What exactly forms a substantial part is a very complex legal question. A few hundred words might not be considered a substantial part of a book, but four lines from a short poem could quite easily be construed as infringing copyright. It is unlikely that a publisher would exact any high penalty from someone who had inadvertently infringed copyright, but it is equally unlikely that a request will be refused – at the worst a small fee may be asked for. The sort of letter to write would go like this:

Copyright Department
Messrs Blank and Blank

Dear Sirs,

The Little Hanbury Theatrical Society, on whose behalf I am writing, will later this year be producing J.M. Barrie's 'Dear Brutus' for three nights in the Clarendon Hall. We are anxious to print in the programme a 300-word extract – which I enclose on a separate sheet – from John Smith's critique of the play which was published by you in 'Barrie: Man and Master'. We would be most grateful for your permission and would of course acknowledge the source of the extract on the programme.

Yours truly,

Letters of reference

John Smith, who lives in a neighbouring town and whom you have known for some years, sends you the following:

> *Dear James,*
>
> *Following my last promotion our finances are in slightly better shape and we have decided that Phyllis is to have some regular help in the house. There is a shortage of suitable people, particularly as the new factory is now offering good rates for part-time work to young women. However, I heard the other day that a year or so ago, when you and Stephanie were living here, you employed a Mrs Brown.*
>
> *I have also heard that she is available and wondered what you – or more particularly Stephanie – thought of her. Do you think she would be suitable for us?*
>
> *With regards to you both,*
>
> *Yours sincerely,*

Now this is not exactly a request for a reference in the accepted sense, but it is the sort of letter which demands the same care and attention in reply as if it were.

The one thing to remember is that when you give a reference, particularly if you feel critical of the person's behaviour or abilities, you can lay yourself open to a charge of defamation if the person written about believes that he or she has been libelled. It is true that in some cases the writer may be able to claim what is called qualified privilege, but to claim this successfully the writer must be able to prove in court the truth of what he/she wrote, and must be able to convince the court that it would have been wrong for him/her to have concealed the facts in the reference. In addition, the writer must be able to prove that his/her statements were not in any way malicious. To the layperson writing a reference it might seem obvious that he would be able to pass all these tests. Maybe he would. But some reference-seekers can be awkward, the law of libel is complex, and it is just as well to avoid the chances of litigation if you can.

It is obvious that the problem only arises when you have something less than wholly good to say about the person concerned, and in this case you have the double problem of being fair to the person who has asked for the reference and of keeping within the law. The situation is made at least slightly less difficult by one convention which is widely accepted and understood. If your reference does not mention an important characteristic (i.e. that the person is honest or a very hard worker) then reading between the lines the recipient can assume that you are unable to vouch for these essential attributes.

To take a case in point. If you had unqualified faith in Mrs Brown's abilities you could reply something like this:

Dear Ronald,

Many thanks for your letter about the lady we still always think of as the admirable Mrs Brown. We certainly think she would be useful to you. Stephanie found her a really hard worker, very anxious to please, and with a very intelligent idea of just what was needed. Also she is extremely honest and very good-tempered. We were both sorry when our move here made it no longer possible for her to come to us regularly.

Yours sincerely,

But the position might not be quite as simple as that and if so this could be a safe but tactfully informative reply:

Dear Ronald,

Many thanks for your letter about Mrs Brown. Yes, we employed her for some months before we moved to Boston, but I find it difficult to say whether she would fit your particular requirements.

I can quite understand that the new factory has absorbed a lot of local labour, but imagine that the situation will not be so desperate when things have settled down.

Yours sincerely,

What you would not say – even if it were true – is: 'Although she was a very good worker, I am afraid that she is a persistent drinker, so keep the cocktail cabinet locked!'

In the same way, if the lady herself wrote to you asking for a reference you would presumably have no difficulty if she was the wonderful person described in the first of the above letters.

If you had not been sorry when a move ended her employment something like this would be satisfactory: 'Mrs Brown was employed by my wife and myself for some months in .... and we found her work satisfactory. We were no longer able to use her services when we moved to this address since the distance from her home was too great for her to travel to us daily.'

Letters making holiday arrangements

Two points should be made about every letter concerned with booking holidays, whether it is a package tour, a suite at a luxury hotel or rooms in a small seaside boarding house. The first is to give *all* the details that are required, and to repeat them in further letters even though this may at first sight seem to be completely unnecessary. Secondly, rigorously check the details before you actually seal the letter and put it in the post.

Leaving out details about matters which you may take for granted but the recipient of your letter may not is a common cause of trouble. So is confusion about dates. It is easier than most of us realize to make a mistake about how many days there are in a month, while June and July are both popular holiday months and with hand-written letters one can easily look like the other.

This is of course one reason for typing rather than writing letters of this sort if possible – and if it is not, then for printing out the important words. Your signature is particularly essential and you should print it in brackets after having written it, like this: *A.J. Smith* (A.J. SMITH). It is also a good reason for confirming bookings in sufficient detail. In other words, not: 'This is to confirm my recent booking', nor even: 'This is to confirm the booking which I made in my letter of May 21st.' What is required is something like this: 'This is to confirm the booking made in my letter of May 21st, for one twin-bedded room plus breakfast from July 8 to July 22 inclusive at the rate of £X per week.'

Booking rooms, either at a hotel or at a guest house, should be simple enough. However, if you are considering staying somewhere that you have never visited before, it is important to ask any questions in your initial letter of enquiry rather than at a later stage. So a first letter could go as follows:

Dear Manager,

Could you please tell me whether you have accommodation for my wife, myself and my 4-year-old son for the fortnight from June 8 to June 22 inclusive?

We would require a twin-bedded room with bathroom – facing the sea if possible – with an adjoining room for my son. We would also need an evening meal as well as breakfast. I would like to know whether a midday meal would be available as and when needed.

Could you also please tell me whether dogs (in this case a Sealyham) are allowed in the bedrooms. I would be grateful to hear whether this is possible, what your rates are and how much deposit is required. Perhaps you could let me know as soon as possible as I am anxious to complete arrangements for the holiday before going abroad on a business trip.

Yours faithfully,

In the preliminary letter you may also want to raise one or two specific matters which are not directly concerned with accommodation. According to circumstances, the following might be mentioned: 'I am a keen fisherman and would be grateful if you could let me have details of any fishing permits required in the area.' Or: 'I am a sailing enthusiast and would be grateful if you would let me have details of where I could hire a boat.'

You should get a reply, if not by return then at least within a week. If this doesn't happen, you could send a brief reminder.

Sometimes the reply will fail to answer the questions you have raised. This may merely be an oversight, but you should not ignore the possibility that it could be a deliberate omission made in the hope that you will not press for an answer and will book the accommodation anyway. So a reply along these lines might be suitable:

Dear Mr Rose,

Thank you for your letter of May 17 in reply to my enquiry of May 13 asking for a twin-bedded room with bathroom for my wife and myself, and another room for my son, from June 8 to June 22 inclusive.

I note that you quote a rate of £X per week for my wife and myself, inclusive of breakfast and evening meal, and of £X per week for my son. Before booking this accommodation I would be grateful if you would answer the points raised in my letter about midday meals and accommodation for our dog.

Yours sincerely,

Booking your own accommodation and your own tickets is only one way of setting about organizing your holiday. An increasing number of holiday-makers prefer to have the entire trip handled by a travel agent, particularly if they are going abroad. If you want an agent to plan and book a tailor-made holiday for you there are certain essential points that you should mention in your letter. After explaining where you want to go, these would be:

1. The number of people travelling in your party.
2. The ages of the children on the day of departure.
3. Length of holiday and dates.
4. Preferred method of travel.
5. The type of accommodation required – self-catering, villa, apartment, hotel.
6. If a hotel, whether you want medium, first or de-luxe class.
7. Does the accommodation provided include any special services, such as the use of a swimming pool, babysitters or sports facilities?
8. Do you prefer the accommodation to be near your point of arrival or a comparatively isolated situation?
9. Is it essential for you to be near a sandy beach?
10. Do you want to be within reasonable distance of a town with (i) good shopping facilities, (ii) good entertainment facilities, (iii) art galleries, museums or buildings of historic interest?
11. Do you require a self-drive car for all or part of your holiday?

12 Do you want to be insured and do you need the agent to help with passports, visas or any inoculations that may be necessary?
13 Do you want a holiday tailor-made to your own requirements, or will you be content with one of the packages they have available?
14 Roughly how much money are you prepared to spend?

If you prefer a package holiday offered by one of the tour operators, the most important point, before you sign anything, is to read the small print in the brochure with extreme care.

If you buy a 'package' holiday from a brochure you will be required to sign the tour operator's booking form and pay a deposit. By doing so you agree to the booking conditions as set out in the brochure, and ignorance of that fact is no defence! Amongst the conditions there will probably be a scale of cancellation fees. So check that your agent or tour operator can provide travel insurance, and pay the premium immediately so that it covers your deposit. Do not wait until the balance is payable on the holiday.

If going to a country with which your country has no reciprocal health arrangements, you will need high medical coverage. If a policy seems inadequate, ring the insurers and check if you can pay an additional premium for higher cover. Be sure to declare to the insurers if you already suffer from an existing disease, such as asthma, for instance, and keep a copy of your letter.

If you fall ill, even with a cold, before the start of your holiday, write and tell the insurers, as this is a condition of most insurance policies. If the cold turns to pneumonia and you have to cancel, the insurers may dispute liability if you have not notified them immediately of any illness, however trivial.

If you have any doubts, raise them in your initial letter of enquiry.

It will not be unreasonable if you ask, before booking, what time the night flight leaves, and what time it arrives. And what time of the day, or early morning, will you arrive at your hotel? Also, what is really included in the 'all-in' price? Do you or the company pay the airport landing charge? And is your baggage handled free? And remember that words mean no more than they say, so that if a hotel is 'within sight of the sea', it would be a good thing to ask how far away it really is. Remember also that in the world of the package tour, as elsewhere, you rarely get more than you pay for.

Having worked your way through the brochures, ask the questions which you feel need answering. Then take a copy, check the dates, and await an acknowledgement.

Complaints

If you have comments on a 'package' booked through an agent with a tour operator (in which case your contract will have been with the latter as principal, not with the agent), you should address a letter to the tour operator, and make two copies.

At the top of the letter give your departure date, the resort, the name of the hotel where you stayed, the length of your stay, the port, airport or station you left from and finally the operator's booking references which you will find on the confirmation invoice. This will help them to find your file easily.

Then outline the cause of your complaint. Be as objective as possible, giving facts rather than opinions. Be accurate and precise and do not include the experiences of other people, however strongly you may feel about them. Remember that it is *your* complaint that is being considered. Attach to your letter photocopies of any receipts or notes that support your case.

You should include all relevant facts but keep the letter as short as possible. If you have taken photographs to support your case, be sure to get extra copies so that should the originals go astray you will still have the evidence.

Send the letter plus one copy to the travel agent and ask the agent to acknowledge receipt and to forward the letter to the tour operator with his covering letter.

The operator should then investigate and reply to you via the agent – not direct. This is the standard practice, since it is assumed that the agent will wish to know how things are progressing even if he is not the principal in the contract.

Other considerations

Once you have booked your holiday, it is important to ensure that your absence won't be obvious to any potential burglars. Here two letters can do a great deal to minimize the risk.

If you have your milk delivered you could write: 'I would be grateful if you would stop deliveries of milk at the above address from June 4th to June 18th inclusive, and resume deliveries as before on the morning of June 19th.'

The second letter should go to your newsagent to cancel deliveries of the daily paper. But here you might wish to add a line or two saying, for instance: 'I do not wish to cancel my orders for "The Economist" or for "The New York Times", and would be glad if you would hold these in your shop until after June 18th when I will collect them personally.'

In both cases you could make a telephone call instead of sending a letter, or go into the shops concerned and give the message verbally. There is, however, a great deal to be said for putting your instructions in writing. If anything goes wrong you can then produce the copy you will have kept to show it was not you who was in the wrong. This is not just typical paranoia but can be very helpful.

It is also important to tell the police your house will be empty. Write to the local police department and, before you do so, find out the name and rank of the officer in charge.

Dear PC Patel,

My wife and I will be taking our annual holiday from July 1 to July 15 inclusive and our house at 15 Burnaby Crescent will be unoccupied for this period, although our friend, Mrs Coates of 7 Burnaby Crescent, will be looking in every few days to see that all is well. I would be most grateful if you could keep a special eye on the house while I am away.

My address from July 1 to 15 will be the Majestic Hotel, Rothesay, telephone number 1243-56789.

Yours sincerely,

If you are lucky enough to have a helpful neighbour who will come into the house during your absence, there will be no need to arrange for correspondence to be forwarded. If not, it is possible to arrange with the mailing office to have your letters re-directed to your holiday address or held at the sorting office until your return.

Before leaving, you will need to remember to turn off water, gas and electricity, unless, that is, you have arranged for a neighbour or friend to come into the house regularly. You should also have checked two important things with your insurance company – or your policy. You *may* find that you are required to let the company know when your house is unoccupied for longer than a certain period. If this is so you should send the company a brief letter telling them the dates between which you will be away. You are, however, rather more likely to find that cover is restricted only if the premises is left unfurnished, the exclusions in such circumstances possibly including theft, burst pipes and malicious damage.

You may also find that your policy stipulates that to keep within the terms of the policy you *must* turn off the water if you leave the house for longer than a specific period. In some cases, this can be as short as a day or two!

Writing to friends

Personal letter writing is becoming something of a lost art, but those who still practise it – or have rediscovered it – can be very pleasantly surprised at the pleasure it brings to both writer and recipient.

People tend to be much less guarded when they write to a friend, feeling they can be as introspective or retrospective as they wish. It is much easier to pour out your heart in a letter than to do it on e-mail, and many people are still uncomfortable with the phone, regarding it as an intrusion and even something of a threat.

A personal letter can be a real reflection of your personality, and when writing to a friend or a member of your family it is better not to make a draft first. Spontaneity should take precedence over perfectly reasoned arguments, unless you are trying to give advice or ask for a commitment. Do not be put off if replies are slow in coming. Most people are procrastinators and delay answering letters for a long time, either being too busy or finding the questions too difficult to answer. A personal letter of this sort could read as follows:

Dear Meeta,

Today I thought of you as I walked in the garden and vividly remembered the holiday and how wonderful it was to meet you. I know we've only been back for a few days but I'm wondering if you would like to come over and have lunch with me one day next week.

If the weather holds, we could eat in the garden and then walk in the countryside. I'd love to show you some of my favourite haunts.

Since my wife died I've become a bit of a loner, and you are the first person with whom I have relaxed for many years. I believe you felt the same way.

I know I'm the first to write but then, as I told you, I'm a natural risk-taker. Do give me a ring and say you'll come.

Yours affectionately,

Ilesh

An invitation like this would be very hard to build up to on the phone, and this is one of the many bonuses of personal letter writing – that you can really express your true feelings without being inhibited by the other person at the end of the line.

In terms of advice, letter writing can also be the best method of communication.

Dear Alan,

I know how much you want to emigrate to Canada and I realize there are many opportunities for you in Quebec. When we talked last you told me your mother was philosophical about your departure – as well as Jean's and the two boys.

Since then, she has telephoned me in considerable distress and, as an old family friend, I think I should pass on to you the stark fact that your mother has been doing an excellent cover up, creating a selfless front as best she can.

I wonder if it would be possible for you to take her with you? She has few friends now and not many roots since your father died. As you are her only child, I thought it right to tell you how she really feels. I hope that you won't feel I'm interfering. Perhaps you could give me a ring and we can have a longer talk on the phone.

With much affection,

Tom

It's difficult to know what Alan's reaction will be, but at least Tom has tried to intercede in the most tactful possible way. By writing a letter he has given Alan the opportunity of mulling the situation over before (or if) he calls. It's not that a letter softens the blow, but it gives an opportunity for the recipient to reflect rather than feel he's being harassed, either by telephone or in person.

Writing a personal letter also presents an ideal way to apologize without embarrassing the recipient or becoming repetitive.

Dear Joe,

I'm so sorry I hurt you in the way I did at the meeting. It was both careless and stupid of me and I have no defence. I do hope my blunder won't affect our friendship.

Sincerely,
Derek

Keeping in touch with friends is important, and if you are busy a postcard (not of the 'wish you were here' variety) is better than the letter you never have time to write.

It's worth buying a selection of these in any newsagent or book store. A pack or a book of 30 cards can range from reproductions of paintings or architecture to photographs and images. A stock of them is very useful and will give great pleasure when received. Here are a couple of examples:

Dear Sarah

I thought the pond you and John are creating in the back garden is most ambitious and will eventually give endless hours of pleasure. Now he has retired, I'm sure John finds time hanging a little heavily on his hands.

Yours, Margaret

Dear Peter

I really enjoyed your talk yesterday. It made me reflect on many aspects of the past, particularly when you discussed tolerance. In many ways you have changed my life.

Yours, Kim

Personal letter writing is one of the most under-estimated of arts and will give you considerable pleasure and stimulation as well as deeper feelings and thoughts.

03 communicating with the authorities

In this chapter you will learn:

- how to write a letter to an authority, such as the gas board or local authority and how to write to your bank
- how to find out the person you should write to
- how to write about building developments
- how to write to the post office with a query or complaint
- how to write to your local government official or MP
- how to write to the police concerning, for example, an abandoned car or an issue of traffic control
- how to express concern about an school incident involving your son or daughter
- about writing to your doctor, or to the church
- how to write to a neighbour about an issue of mutial concern, such as parking
- how to request an estimate for work to your house – and how to complain when that work is unsatisfactory
- how to make an insurance claim
- how to write a letter of apology

Writing to any authority, whether it is about water rates, electricity, gas or the local authorities, is a depressing task, but it's amazing how much red tape can be cut through by a simple and concise letter.

First of all, remember that a letter to the authorities should be formal in tone. Secondly, the correspondence may have to be passed around from one office to another, and its smallest point commented on or examined in detail. You should therefore ensure even more carefully than usual that what you say is accurate, to the point and brief. Make sure you keep a proper copy of what you have said, i.e. a carbon copy or a photocopy which you can take on machines at many newsagents and public libraries throughout the country.

Since your letter, whether it is a request for information or a complaint, will be of at least a semi-official nature, you should not introduce personal aspects unless these are directly relevant to the subject.

The Secretary, the Chairman, or the Departmental Officer may be known to you, but you should never end an official letter with anything like 'I hope we shall see you at our normal reunion at the end of the month', or 'I see that your son James has now started attending the same school as Christopher.' Quite apart from the fact that such comments have nothing to do with the matter in hand, there can always be the suspicion that you are trying to gain preferential treatment from a friend.

To whom should you write?

At the top of most authorities' notepaper you will see an instruction such as: 'Letters to be addressed to the Director' or 'All communications to be made to the Secretary'. Keep to this.

While this practice of writing to an impersonal 'Secretary' or 'Director' is usually correct when dealing with the bigger organizations, there are sometimes exceptions – for instance when making a complaint to a gas company or a firm of manufacturers – where one person in the organization may have the task of dealing with letters of this kind. In this case, find out who the person is, and write to them directly by name.

When trying to find out exactly which organization to write to for a given problem, you can very often find the answer at your local library. The reference sections of most libraries are huge mines of information. On their shelves you will find books or booklets which give details of your local council, and others providing information about local businesses and industries. If you can't find the address of the local planning authority, for instance, the chances are that the library staff will be able to help you.

Development schemes

New roads and new buildings are the most frequent causes of a change in the environment likely to affect the value of a house, and you may well wish to get as much advance information as possible on such proposed changes. If you have heard rumours of new developments, first find from your local Zoning Board or Town Hall or, failing that, from the public library, the name and address of the local Planning Officer. Then write as follows:

Dear Mr Raven,

As the owner and occupier of No 15 Sykes Avenue I have been disturbed to hear reports that a nine-story apartment block is to be built on the plot of empty land between Number 24 and Number 30 Charteris Street. As you know, Sykes Avenue backs on to Charteris Street and a block of this height built on the plot would inevitably be detrimental to the amenities of No 15 as it would cut off a great deal of light as well as having an overpowering effect. I should be most grateful if you would let me know whether this report is true.

Yours sincerely,

It is advisable in this type of correspondence to exercise a certain amount of caution in your approach. Although you may feel certain that your information is reliable, there is always the possibility of a mistake and you lose nothing by writing in guarded terms to start with. To say that you 'have heard it reported' gives you an escape route if you have been misinformed while paving the way for further letters if these are found to be necessary.

In today's complex world, even the most conscientious official may not be fully informed of what is going on. You might receive a reply telling you that as far as he is aware there are no plans for the erection of an apartment block in your area, and that he is certain that no permission has yet been granted. You may not feel convinced; in which case you will have to extend your enquiries and do a bit more detective work. After this you may be able to follow up with something along these lines:

Dear Mr Raven,

You may remember that I wrote to you on May 24 regarding reports that a nine-story apartment block was to be built on the vacant plot of land between Number 24 and Number 30 Charteris Street, and you replied that planning permission had not been granted. I see from the June issue of 'Building News', a cutting from which I enclose, that the Chairman of ... recently announced an extension of growth and referred to 'an ambitious plan for new units south of Main Street in Charteris Street'.

I would be grateful to know if the position has changed since you last wrote to me.

Yours sincerely,

In all such letters it is essential that no accusations should be made against anyone, even by implication. You should also remember that plans for virtually all major developments legally have to be made available to the public for a certain period during which objections can be made. So get as much information as you can as soon as you can.

The mail

If you have a suggestion, a query or a complaint about your mail, you should write to your head postmaster. You can find out who this is by asking at your post office or by looking them up in a telephone directory.

In all dealings with the Post Office – as with most other authorities – sweet reasonableness, an attitude of more-in-sorrow-than-in-anger, will often produce results where anger could be less effective. You should not, therefore, write: 'I was astounded to arrive home tonight to find that a parcel addressed to me here, and containing valuable photographs, had been tossed into the basement area of the house where it stayed for some hours in the rain before being noticed. The packet was naturally too large to be put through our small letterbox, but my wife was at home all day and no attempt whatsoever was made to deliver the package by hand. The service provided by the Post Office is disgraceful.'

There are a number of things wrong with such a letter. There is no reason to say that you were astounded. The fact that you are writing is enough evidence of this. There is no point in admitting that you have a letterbox too small to take packets of the sort you are presumably used to receiving. The Post Office has for years been pointing out that larger letterboxes make delivering the mail less difficult. You do not, of course, *have* to fit one, but there is no reason for pointing out that you have not done so. The claim that 'no attempt' was made may be correct, but even the postman's knock can be missed, and it would be unwise to claim that he or she had deliberately shirked their job unless you had evidence that this was so. As for the last sentence it is clear from your complaint that you believe the service to be disgraceful and there is no need to repeat it.

A far more fruitful way of presenting your complaint would be to write something along these lines:

Dear Sir/Madam

I found on my arrival home here tonight that a packet brought by the postman this morning had been thrown into the basement area where it remained in the rain until being discovered some hours later. The postman does not appear to have knocked – my wife was in the house all day – and I assume that he thought the house was empty. The packet contained valuable photographs which could have been irreparably damaged, and I should be grateful if you would ensure that the same thing does not happen again.

Yours faithfully,

Your local government official or MP

It is often the local government official Member of Parliament to whom a final appeal is made if a complaint is a serious one, and their post-bag contains a fairly high percentage of letters dealing with complaints which no one else has been able to handle satisfactorily.

Many of these letters consist of criticisms about the inefficiency, or alleged inefficiency, of government departments where officialdom is thought to have fallen down on its job. The rules, as always, are simple: be brief, be clear, and give as much factual information as possible.

Dear Joan Parsons,

I am writing as one of your constituents for more than ten years on a subject which I feel will concern you.

I'm referring to the general deterioration in the environmental standards of the Bicklin Hill area.

When my wife and I moved to the above address in 1987, it was situated in a quiet residential area. Since then there have been considerable changes. The new town by-pass, which now comes to within 100 yards of the northern edge of Bicklin Hill, has forced many residents to leave the area. As a result, many of the houses have been converted into blocks of one-room apartments which house a constantly changing population.

This increase in the number of inhabitants has put additional strain on the over-worked refuse disposal services. As a result some of the streets now have an appearance that would have been unthinkable a few years ago.

An increasing number of houses are empty for longish periods, and while the police do what they can, this makes their job difficult.

I do not think that blame for the situation should be laid entirely on the refuse disposal service. It seems to me that there are a number of causes. I'm sure you, as our local representative, might be able to help to prevent the situation getting worse. No one wants the Bicklin Hill area to deteriorate into a slum.

Yours sincerely,

The police department

The police have always taken the view that the public can help them in their work, so have no hesitation in writing to them, first finding out the name of the officer in charge.

Dear Inspector Wright,

Although curtains are still hanging in the front room of No 13 Cedar Drive, which backs on to my home, the house has been unoccupied for some months. Now that the leaves of the creeper have fallen it is possible to see that one of the back kitchen windows is open which could well invite burglars.

I thought I should draw your attention to the situation.

Yours sincerely,

Abandoned cars can be another problem:

Dear Officer Wilson

A red Scorpio licence plate ... has been standing for the last five weeks on the disused plot at the end of the rcad leading from the southern end of Main Street towards the park. The car appears to be new.

Yours sincerely,

Another serious problem is traffic control:

Dear Inspector Wright,

I am writing on behalf of many parents in the area who have children attending the new school at Elm Road. As you will know this is virtually outside the town and is, I understand, beyond the area where the traffic patrol normally operates.

Most of the children come from the southern part of the town. There is also a large number who have to cross Parkside. This has always been a busy road and now, following the opening of the new highway, is used as a short cut around the west side of the town by an increasing number of heavy commercial lorries and private cars.

The nearest pedestrian crossing is some way up the road from the school, and while children are encouraged to use it, many do not. It is not always possible for parents to deliver and collect children and it is worrying to think of them unsupervised on an extremely dangerous stretch of road.

I know that you are short-staffed, but am nevertheless asking whether it would be possible for you to station an officer outside the school when the children are arriving and going home.

Yours sincerely,

Such a letter could, of course, have been sent – written in a slightly different way – to the head or principal of the school concerned.

Schoolboards and educational authorities

The simplest letters are those which deal with the academic progress – or lack of it – of a son or daughter. How you start your letter will to some extent be governed by how well you know the Principal or Head Teacher.

In such letters there is no point in trying to disguise what you really want to say with diplomatic wording, such as: 'In some ways my wife and I feel that our son John has not quite reached the levels which we had expected him to reach by the age of twelve.' The following would be more direct:

Dear Mr/Mrs Palmer,

My son John, who is now aged ten, has been at Grove Elementary for three years and my wife and I are worried by his lack of progress in maths. While he reads better than most boys of his age, and appears to be extremely well informed on matters of general knowledge, his lack of ability to do even the simplest sums is worrying.

I have no reason to think that this is the fault of the teacher and am wondering whether it is due to lack of interest in figures or laziness. My own feeling is that it may be lack of interest due to his feeling that however hard he tries he is bound to get the work wrong.

I would be most grateful if you would tell us what we could do at home to help improve his performance.

Yours sincerely,

Rather more difficult is the letter to a Principal or Head Teacher in which you wish to protest about some incident at school. A spur-of-the-moment letter can often produce problems:

Dear Mr Talbot,

I was shocked when I came home tonight to learn that my son John arrived home from school today with a badly cut hand. Apparently it was injured while he was in the school playground this morning. Although we have not taken him to the doctor – he says that he was given some first aid at school – I am astounded that there was no proper supervision. I would like to hear from you at once as I intend taking the matter further.

Now this letter includes almost every mistake that a parent could make in the circumstances. Firstly, there is really no need to explain when you heard of the incident. The relevant point is that it happened. Was John's hand 'badly cut'? The fact that you have not considered it necessary to take him to the doctor suggests that this is not so. Was there really a lack of supervision in the playground? Accidents can happen anywhere and, after all, you have only heard your son's story and he is hardly an unbiased witness. The last sentence seems a clear indication that you intend making yourself as awkward as possible even though you have only a very incomplete version of what happened.

The following letter should produce results:

Dear Mr Talbot,

My son John arrived home from school this afternoon with a bad cut on his right hand which he tells us was the result of an accident in the school playground. I gather that this was treated at school and am grateful that this was done. However, I am rather worried that accidents of this type can take place. My wife and I are wondering what exactly the circumstances were. If you could find time to let us know, we would be grateful.

Yours sincerely,

This letter should bring an explanatory reply. However, if it doesn't or there is a reply that is negative such as: 'I really see no need to discuss the very minor accident to which you refer', try writing as follows:

Dear Mr Talbot,

I have received no reply to my letter of May 4 (copy enclosed), and although I appreciate that at this time of year you will have even more work to deal with than usual, nevertheless, I would appreciate a reply soon.

Yours sincerely,

The 'copy enclosed' is always useful in such cases since it prevents the recipient of your letter pleading that the first letter must have gone astray and wasting time by asking you to repeat the contents.

If a Principal or Head Teacher fails to give details, your reaction will depend on how far you are really determined to push the matter. But first of all give them the chance to change their mind.

Dear Mr Talbot,

I am sorry to learn from your letter of May 7 that you feel there is no need to give me any information on the circumstances of my son's accident in your school on May 4. I quite understand how busy you are, but feel that in this case you have not fully appreciated the implications of what has happened. I am reluctant to take the matter up elsewhere and hope that you will be able to let me have some explanation of the incident.

Yours sincerely,

This may, of course, produce another evasive answer. If it does, you should complain to the school board or County Education Officer.

Rather more difficult to write is the letter to the school board or local education authority when you move into a new area. You will want your children to receive the best education that the area can offer, but so will other parents, and if there are not enough 'good' places to go round, a lot will depend on how you deal with the situation. As a start you should write to the Chief Education Officer or President of the local school board with a letter that could go something like this:

Dear Mrs Staples,

I shall be moving from the above address in London into The Limes, Bury Street, Tadchester, on October 15, together with my wife and two children, John aged 12 and Judy aged 13. John has been attending the Winklehurst Comprehensive School in Ealing and Judy the Ealing High School for Girls. Both these schools have an excellent academic record.

I am naturally anxious that their education should be continued with as little disruption as possible, and I am hoping that you will be able to supply me with details of suitable schools in the area so that I can write to them directly.

I look forward to hearing from you.

Yours truly,

Doctors

A letter to your doctor falls into a special category, and it is quite likely you will have to write one or more of them at various intervals throughout your life.

Before suggesting ways of handling this kind of correspondence, it is worth mentioning a formal letter that many people forget. If you change your address, even though you are still living in the same area, your doctor should be informed. A letter should go something like this:

Dear Dr Jones,

I have been your patient for the last three years at the above address, but shall be moving on September 15 to 4 Acacia Buildings, where my telephone number will be 9876-54321. Unless I hear to the contrary, I shall assume that I will still be in the right area for your practice.

Yours sincerely,

Letters to your doctor can cover an enormous range of subjects. Try to put the basic facts in the first paragraph; next, go on to what is wrong, or what advice you are needing. This is a typical example:

Dear Dr Jones,

Six months ago, after discussion with you, I began taking the oral contraceptive ... I have now decided to stop taking these pills and would like to know whether I should call upon you for further advice. To save you the trouble of replying, I will telephone the practice receptionist within the next few days.

Yours sincerely,

While this is the kind of brevity which will help a busy person, all good doctors feel that their patients should be able to write to them confidentially, without inhibitions. There may well be matters that a patient would prefer to put down in a preliminary letter before having a talk with the doctor. If so, a longer letter would be justified. For example, if the problem is a psychological one, it could well help the doctor if he had the opportunity of digesting a long letter before he met the patient to discuss the problem personally.

There are, of course, an infinitely large number of variations between the 'brief' and the 'long rambling' letter, but before sitting down to write to your doctor, ask yourself this question: 'What does he really want to know before he can help me?'

There are some occasions on which it is difficult to know whether a letter is preferable to a telephone call, and this is often so when advice is sought about an elderly relative. If you feel a letter is necessary, it should be written particularly carefully:

Dear Dr James,

You will see from your records that my father, Mr Jonathan Smith of the above address, has had only very minor illnesses since he became your patient nearly 20 years ago. However, during the last few weeks he has lost his appetite, appears to have numerous 'aches and pains', and seems to be increasingly tired after the slightest exertion.

He maintains that there is nothing wrong with him, and his troubles may be largely due to the fact that he is now 81. I would, however, be extremely grateful if you could call on him so that we can be sure there is nothing radically wrong. To save you the trouble of replying, I will give your practice receptionist a telephone call within the next few days.

Yours sincerely,

There are many occasions on which you may want your doctor to sign a form for you, e.g. absence from work, taking out an insurance policy, or the need for a note about your general health which is required for a prospective employer. Any letter requesting a doctor's signature should always state a willingness to pay a fee for it.

Dear Dr Jones,

I would be extremely grateful if you would sign the enclosed form dealing with ... I am of course prepared to pay your fee for this.

Yours sincerely,

The church

The three events about which people are most likely to write to their local religious official are births, marriages and deaths. While it is possible to telephone and ask for an appointment about a christening, a brief preliminary letter is a good idea.

Dear Mr Birch,

I am anxious that my son, Jeremy John, who was born a week ago, should be christened in the church which both my wife and I attend and should be grateful if we could make arrangements for this when convenient.

To save you the trouble of replying, I will give you a telephone call within the next few days.

Yours sincerely,

Marriage requests can be complicated by previous divorce. The important thing is to give the facts briefly.

Dear Mr Jamieson,

I am engaged to be married to Mrs Kingsley-Smith who is a resident of your parish. She is anxious that we should be married in church and I would be most grateful if you could arrange to see us both in the not too distant future. I should point out that Mrs Kingsley-Smith was divorced from her husband three years ago.

Yours sincerely,

Off-street parking

With some residents having to pay substantial sums to park their cars outside their own houses, there is a good deal to be said for seeing whether the space between detached or semi-detached houses can be used for this purpose. To take this up with the local authority means first communicating with your neighbours, which can often need full United Nations-style diplomacy.

Before any such letter is written, the following points should be carefully considered:

- Have you got as much information as you can get about the person to whom you are writing?
- Are you putting forward a tentative proposal about which you want agreement in principle?
- Are you offering at least a partly cut-and-dried proposition?
- Have you done the necessary homework?

The first step is to establish the name and initials of the neighbour and whether or not he or she has a car! Next visit the Town Hall to discover from the Planning Officer whether there are any bye-laws covering the construction of drives and garages.

Most local authorities are anxious to encourage off-street parking. Nevertheless, there will be some legal points to be considered since both you and your neighbour will have to give each other right-of-way. The next step is an estimate of what the change will cost. Once you have got that, you can write a letter which you hope will gain your neighbour's co-operation.

Dear Mr Bates,

As the new owner of Whitecroft I have already discovered the difficulty of local parking, and I gather that the Residents' Parking Permit, although costing £.. a year, gives no guarantee that you can park near your own house.

I imagine that you suffer from the same problem and I am wondering whether you would be interested in discussing some plan whereby the slip-ways between your house and mine might be converted into asingle, wider drive giving access to our back gardens.

I understand that there are no local bye-laws which would rule this out.

My family and I will not be moving into our new home for several weeks as we are having various alterations made, but I shall be visiting the house at the weekends.

If the idea interests you, perhaps you could drop me a line.

Yours sincerely,

Your neighbour may have reservations, but a letter such as the above does not suggest that he should commit himself and is simply a discussion document. You might expect the following reply:

Dear Mr Lavender,

Thank you for your letter regarding the local parking problem and a possible solution. I am certainly interested although I have certain reservations: I am not sure that I am anxious to lose a part of the garden, even for the car. Also, I am not certain about the cost that would be involved, or how it would affect the value of our houses. If you are visiting the house next Saturday, perhaps you and your wife would like to drop in for a drink.

Yours sincerely,

Requests for estimates

For any sizeable job that involves repairing and decorating your house, it is important to ask for a written estimate:

Dear Mr Loveday,

Please could you let me have an estimate for painting the front of my house. I would include in this the windows of both storeys, the front door and the small portion of stucco work which covers the front of the house to the first storey.

I would like this work to be carried out as soon as possible.

Yours sincerely,

When you receive the estimate you should check it carefully, and in particular the number of coats of paint which your house will be given.

Complaints

It is always better to complain on paper and to be absolutely sure of your facts.

The letter to avoid is this: 'Dear Sirs, It is only six weeks since your men finished the work of adding a bathroom to this house and already there are cracks appearing in the plaster. I told them at the time that they were doing the job in a very slap-dash way and this is the result. What is more, some of the tiles you fitted at such great cost are coming away, and although I have tried there seems to be nothing I can do to fix them. The window is also jamming badly. Unless all these things are put right immediately there will be serious trouble.'

This letter contains almost every example of the wrong approach. 'Cracks appearing in the plaster' is a common complaint, but in fact some minor settlement frequently takes place and while you might be justified in raising the issue this is not the way to do so. The second sentence has two errors. The writer has made an important grammatical error and implies that the cracks are the result of his reprimand and not of slap-dash workmanship. If he really wanted to make this point he should have said: 'This is the result of very slap-dash workmanship about which I spoke to the men at the time.' Next, it is no good complaining about the 'great cost' of the tiles since you presumably agreed to this before the work began. Nor is it wise to admit that you yourself have 'tried' to put matters right. You might, in fact, lay yourself open to charges of creating the problem yourself. New windows sometimes do jam, and while this is certainly a cause for complaint, it can probably be rectified without difficulty and is certainly no excuse for the implied threat. Finally, if by 'serious trouble' the writer means that the firm will have legal action taken against it, this is entirely the wrong way of saying so.

The complaint should read as follows:

Dear Sir/Madam,

Cracks are now appearing in the plaster of the bathroom which you completed at the above address six weeks ago. I would like to know the cause of this and also when it will be possible for you to carry out the further re-plastering required. At the same time I would be glad if your staff would replace a number of the bathroom tiles which have unaccountably come away. The new window you fitted is jamming so badly that it is impossible to open without a great deal of effort.

I trust that you will be able to make good these defects without delay and that no further action will be necessary on my part.

Yours faithfully,

Similar care should be exercised in any letter of complaint. It is always a good idea to get a rough estimate before, for instance, leaving a television or a lawn-mower for repair.

Again, the letter to avoid is as follows: 'When I left my lawn-mower with you a fortnight ago I never expected that you would do so much work on it. I thought that all it needed was a new spark plug, change of oil, etc., and now I get a bill for more than £100, which I have no intention of paying.'

It is obvious from the first sentence that there was no clear agreement as to how much work would be needed on the machine, and in the circumstances the repairer would probably be successful if he attempted to sue for the money.

If you have to deal with unsatisfactory verbal agreements, you may decide either that the repairer is 'trying it on', or that he has made a genuine mis-estimate of how much time has been spent on the job. It would be extremely dangerous to imply that he was guilty of 'trying it on' and your letter, which must unfortunately be written from a position of weakness, should go something like this:

Dear Sir/Madam,

Thank you for your bill for £100 for repairing the lawn-mower which I left with you a fortnight ago. I am wondering, however, if there has been some error. I gather from the parts which you list under 'materials', that you felt something more than a change of oil and a new spark plug was required, but I feel that a mistake has been made under the cost of 'labour'.

I appreciate that costs are continually rising, but having had work recently carried out elsewhere on a garden cultivator, I would be glad of your comments on the bill, which I am returning.

Yours faithfully,

A conciliatory reply could be along the following lines:

Dear Sir/Madam,

The lawn-mower to which you refer in your letter of June 10 did in fact need considerably more work than you anticipated if it was to give satisfactory service during the coming season.

However, I am prepared to reduce the total bill by £25 and am enclosing an amended invoice.

Yours faithfully,

No admission has been made of over-charging and it is no doubt hoped that the customer will not only pay up but come again.

If a dispute arises you can contact your local Consumer Advice and Trading Standards offices or the Better Business Bureau. These are run by the local authorities. The staff at the offices will be able to explain the latest rules and regulations which, while giving the consumer increased protection, are sometimes considered rather complicated. Citizens Advice Bureaux could also help here.

Whether your first step should be to go back to the shop or to visit the local authority centre will depend on the complexity of the case, the amount of money involved, and whether or not you feel that a genuine mistake has been made.

Only after you have done your best at the shop should you put your complaint in writing. If you bought goods for cash, write to the supplier, which in most cases will be the shop; if you bought them on Hire Purchase, write to the finance company involved.

In either case, write to the chair or managing director, and if possible find out his or her name. Your letter should start by putting down the facts simply and accurately. Next you should describe what went wrong. Alternatively, if the article is not defective but different from its description, you would have to point this out. There should then follow the most important part of the letter which asks for return of your money. Do not forget to keep a copy, and send the letter by recorded delivery.

Your letter might go like this:

Dear Mr Sparks,

On March 15, 19.., I bought a Mark II ... refrigerator from ... at a cost of £.... Within forty-eight hours of installation, the refrigerator ceased to operate, and I understand from the electrician who came to inspect the machine that the trouble is due to a faulty motor which will have to be replaced. Your firm have refused to do this.

I understand that the transaction is covered by legislation, and am looking to your company for a return of the price paid within 14 days.

Yours faithfully,

The time given to the vendor is a matter for the buyer to choose, but 14 days is considered reasonable. If this first letter fails to bring a satisfactory reply a reminder such as the following should be sent:

Dear Sir/Madam,

I have had no reply to my letter of May 4 (copy enclosed) dealing with the purchase of a Mark II ... refrigerator from ... and would be glad of a reply without further delay, or I may have to consider legal action.

Yours faithfully,

If this produces no result you can then employ a solicitor to take the matter further. Before doing so you would be well advised to consult the Consumer Advice or Better Business Bureau office again, or the Citizens Advice Bureau. The reason is that claims up to £500 can be handled by the Small Claims Court, without you necessarily incurring the expense of using a lawyer.

Insurance claims

Making a claim of any sort can be equally complex, but whether the claim follows a burglary, storm damage to your house or any other incident against which it is possible to insure, the rule is: *Read the insurance policy before you start to make the claim.*

The most obvious mistake would be to claim for something that is not covered by the policy, or is perhaps even specifically excluded. Under some policies, the holder pays a first specified amount of the excess, and under others pays a percentage. If you have sustained £100 of damage to the roof of a house and have to pay the first £100 of any claim, there is no point in making one, particularly as many insurance companies operate a system which provides free cover to non-claimants once in every so many years. In the case of small losses, you should consider carefully whether it is worth making a claim at all.

Assuming that your policy covers the incident and that you intend to make a claim, make sure you telephone the insurer to find out whether you need to complete a claim form. If so, you don't have to write a letter at all. Assuming, however, that this is not so, and that a letter is necessary, write without delay.

The following should be sufficient:

> *Dear Sir/Madam,*
>
> *I wish to make a claim under my Policy No 1234/567 for damage caused to the roof of this house during the storm on the night of September 3/4. The high winds lifted the tiles at the north-east corner of the roof, shifting them and allowing in the torrential rain that accompanied the wind. As a result, much of the plaster ceiling in one bedroom has collapsed, and it appears from inspection by a local builder that most of the ceiling will have to be replastered. The builder, Mr _ of... estimates that the cost of this will be £X*

I also wish to make a claim under Policy No 123333/567 for damage to the carpet and bedding in the room, most of which will have to be replaced. I estimate the cost of this to be £X

Yours faithfully,

A more difficult kind of insurance letter is the one which must be written following a motor car accident. It is notorious that six honest eye-witnesses can give six contradictory accounts of the same accident, and it is most important that in writing to your insurance company you should be as accurate as possible in separating fact from opinion.

An inadequate letter would run as follows: 'Driving from London along Knightsbridge two days ago a car some way ahead of me suddenly turned round, without making any signals at all, trying to make a U-turn. I naturally ran into it and the driver blamed me for not taking care, although it was of course entirely his own fault. He says he is Mr John Jones of ... and I think it absolutely scandalous that he should be driving at all and causing accidents of this sort. His car was hardly damaged but my near-side wing is stove in, the headlamp wrecked and I should think the car would also need a new bumper as I doubt if the existing one can be straightened out.'

This driver could have a very good case, but his letter presents it in the worst possible way. He has waited two days before writing to the insurance company but he still seems incoherent with rage. The best way of writing the letter is as follows:

Dear Sir/Madam,

I was driving east in the right-hand lane along the Brompton Road at 2.30 pm on Sunday, May 4th, at about 25 miles an hour. Traffic was slight. The weather was clear but the roads were slippery from a recent heavy shower of rain.

While passing the main entrance to Harrods I noticed, some 30 yards ahead of me and driving slowly in the same direction in the left-hand lane, a yellow Volvo (registration ...).

The Volvo was moving at little more than walking pace but suddenly, and without any warning, made a sharp right turn, apparently as part of a U-turn. On reaching the right-hand, east-ward bound lane, the driver was prevented from continuing his U-turn by traffic moving in the west-bound lanes. I braked as hard as was possible and, on approaching the Volvo, pulled hard down on my right-hand lock so that I hit the vehicle at an angle rather than head-on.

The damage to the Volvo appeared to consist of no more than a couple of dents in the off-side door panel but the wing of my car (registration ..., covered by your Policy No ...) was badly damaged, the headlamp wrecked and the fender will require replacement.

The driver, who gave his name and address as ... and his Insurance Company as the ..., asked why I had not seen him. I replied that I had seen him but that he had given no warning whatsoever of his move. He made no reply.

Mrs ... of ... who stopped after seeing the impact says that she saw the Volvo start its U-turn but does not recollect seeing any warning sign. U-turns are forbidden on this stretch of road.

Yours faithfully,

Many kinds of insurance claim can involve writing to solicitors but this is not necessarily difficult or complicated. In most cases, you will initially be asking only for an interview. Having made your request, all that is needed is to set down a brief summary of what you want to discuss.

Dear Mrs Jackson,

I am seeking advice concerning a clause in the will of my father who died abroad some weeks ago. I would be grateful for an appointment with you.

Yours sincerely,

Banking

Much the same formula applies to most letters to your bank. In general it is best to be brief and to the point.

Dear Mrs Jones,

I would be glad of a short discussion about my financial affairs and will telephone your secretary within the next few days for a mutually convenient time.

I wish to add a small extension to the house at the above address which I own freehold. The estimated cost is about .... and I would like your advice on the best way of financing this.

Yours sincerely,

The information will allow the Bank Manager not only to study your statements for the last few years but consider them in the specific light of the matter you have raised.

Errors in bank statements should be dealt with at once.

Dear Mrs Jones,

I notice that on page 23 of my statement which I received today, a sum of £53 has been credited to my account apparently in error. As you will see from your records I have not paid in this amount during the period covered. Please confirm a correction has been made.

Yours sincerely,

Apologies

Admitting that you are wrong is never easy and your letter should be short and to the point.

Dear Mr Smith,

Thank you for your letter of the 14th May. I now realize what the position is, and see that the mistake was mine and not yours. I hope you will accept my apologies.

Yours sincerely,

A letter of apology also applies if you have forgotten to do something that you promised to do, and there is a brief but useful routine that you should go through before you put any letter in the post. Read it through once more to see if there is anything in it about which you should make a note.

If you have promised to put something in the post unless you hear from your correspondent within a week, note a reminder of this in your diary several days ahead. If you have said 'I will give you a telephone call within the next few days', then jot down a note to make that call.

If you *have* made a mistake, be honest and apologize.

Dear Mr White,

I am writing to you with many apologies. You will remember that in my letter to you earlier this month, asking for advice about buying some furniture, I said that I would telephone you within a few days.

Unfortunately, I was unexpectedly called away on business and was unable to contact you.

Yours sincerely,

The reverse of an apology is called for if you have received a letter obviously intended for someone else but put into an envelope addressed to you. Here something as brief as possible is required, such as:

Dear Mr Green,

I have just received the enclosed letter which has been addressed to me in error, so I am returning it herewith.

Yours sincerely,

Children's clubs

Nowadays, any parent needs to be reassured that a children's club or camp is safely run with good organization and programming. This could range from a playgroup to a youth club, or from the scouts and guides to an adventure holiday. If a brochure is available, study it carefully to ensure that the instructors/carers are properly qualified and have a programme that is going to fully occupy the child.

In the case of a youth organization the following letter could apply. Don't forget to mention if there is anything special about your child and his or her needs.

Dear Mrs Mason,

My son, Derek, is very keen to join your youth club but before he does I would be grateful if you could answer these questions:

1 Is the club supervised at all times?

2 Could you let me have a programme of activities?

3 Derek suffers from asthma. He is a football enthusiast

and is used to giving himself a dose of his Ventolin spray when required. Can I leave a spare spray with you or your colleagues in case he loses his own?

Thank you so much.

Yours sincerely,

If your child is going to join a camp or go on an adventure holiday, the following would be relevant:

Dear Mr Hardy,

My daughter is looking forward to her adventure training holiday with your organization. Could you very kindly answer these questions:

1 Are all your instructors fully qualified?
2 Could you let me see a programme of activities?
3 Are the children supervised at night?
4 Is it possible for her to phone home?
5 As the result of a car accident, she has a slight limp. She is perfectly fit but self-conscious about the limp. Could you let your staff know about this without drawing attention to the matter publicly?

Thank you so much.

Yours sincerely,

At the opposite end of the age range, there are letters that need to be written either by an elderly person or by their friends or relatives.

Dear Mr Chambers,

My mother, Eileen Farrell, is currently leading a rather lonely existence despite the support of myself and my sister. She is very independent but recently suffered a fall and has lost confidence.

She is aware of the problem and would like to visit your centre a couple of days a week. Could you let me know what kind of programme is available? My mother is very fit and healthy for her age and has no special needs.

Yours sincerely,

In the case of accommodation where a warden is on duty, the following letter might be a first step:

Dear Mrs Ascot,

My parents, Jane and Arthur Burton, are now in their late seventies and finding their present large house difficult to run. My mother has a heart condition and my father has arthritis. Both are fully ambulant and want to be as independent as possible.

Could you let me know the procedures about applying for a flat at Willow Court? Could you also let me have some idea of the cost of purchasing one of the flats?

Thank you so much.

Yours sincerely,

If an elderly person needs welfare assistance or help from the relevant social department, it is much better to visit their offices initially rather than writing a letter.

04 business letters

In this chapter you will learn:

- how to write a business letter, including a job application, a letter requesting a reference and a letter of resignation
- how to give a written reprimand and write a letter of dismissal
- how to write an effective sales letter
- how to write letters concerning overdue payments and orders
- how to report meetings
- about writing abroad and in particular about how to write business letters concerning buying and selling abroad
- about filling in forms.

Job applications

Of all the letters that you are ever likely to write under the heading of 'business', one of the most important will be when applying for a job. A well-written letter will not guarantee that you get the job but, on the other hand, a poor letter goes a long way towards ensuring failure, however good your qualifications may be, so it's important to give a great deal of thought to what you want to say.

What you need to do is draw up a CV (Curriculum Vitae), which should give some biographical notes, academic achievements and other jobs you have done.

The CV should start with your educational background. If you are in your late teens it is relevant to list your school record, exam passes and the subjects in which they were gained. If you are in your late twenties or more it may seem strange to your prospective employer. He is more interested in what you have achieved during the past few years. However, any university degrees, diplomas or any technical or professional qualifications should be mentioned, even if they are not directly relevant.

Achievements which have a direct relation to the job should be stated, although a word of warning is needed here. If you are a very young man applying for a post with a firm which manufactures sporting equipment, it will be useful if you can mention that you captained your school cricket Eleven. If, however, you are in your thirties, it would be advisable to consider whether your prospective employer might not regard this as a sign of backward thinking. It would probably be best left to the interview.

If you are applying for your first job, your letter is comparatively easy since you do not have to describe your present work. If you are already employed, however, it is essential that you give an adequate account of what you are doing. 'At present I work for one of the directors of Williams & Sons' is not very informative. More useful would be a sentence which said: 'For the last three years I have been employed by Williams & Sons, have worked for the director who has special responsibility for exports, and am therefore accustomed to communicating with customers in Europe and Asia.' Here, of course, you should refer to your proficiency in any foreign languages. Be honest, however, and remember that 'fluent French' or 'a good working knowledge of French' should not be an exaggeration. It would also be useful if you could say, for instance: 'I have a good working knowledge of French, written and spoken. As regards the latter, I spent three months, two years ago, living with a family in Rouen.'

In listing your personal qualifications there are good and bad ways of doing this. A bad letter would run like this: 'When I went to Paterson and Company four years ago I was merely a junior assistant to the Research Director. He discovered, however, that I was particularly good at handling people and within 18 months I was put in charge of a section with a dozen employees. Since then I have been promoted to have control of a second section and now have two dozen employees, both women and men, working for me.'

To take the last point first, the employees are not, in fact, working for you but working for the company. Also, while you may have stated the facts accurately, your letter betrays an ego which might well make an employer think 'I wonder if she'll cause trouble with my staff.'

You could give the same information, and create a much better impression if you wrote this: 'I joined Paterson and Company four years ago as an assistant to the Research Director, was subsequently put in charge of a small section in the laboratory and am now in charge of two sections with a total of 24 employees.'

A potential employer who had read the details of what you are doing at present will then naturally ask: 'Why is this person leaving?' There may be a perfectly reasonable answer to this, and if so you should put it down, accurately but briefly, early in your letter. You might, for instance, be able to say: 'I am answering your advertisement as Paterson and Company, for whom I am working at present, are moving their factory to the north of England and I do not wish to leave London.' If you can supplement this by an additional explanation, such as '... because I do not wish to disrupt my children's education', that will help to banish the idea that you are a stick-in-the-mud with a dislike for mobility. Or there might be another reason, such as: 'There is little chance of Paterson and Company expanding in the near future and I am looking for a fresh appointment because of the lack of promotion prospects.'

Another possibility is that you have got the sack, or been made redundant. In times of depression and contracting trade, being made redundant does not carry the stigma that it would in other circumstances. There is no point in hiding the fact in your letter of application. It will almost certainly come to light if you are successful in gaining an interview, and it is unlikely to count as a black mark against you if this explanation is given: 'I have been made redundant after six years at Paterson due to the contraction of their business and their decision to close one of the factories.'

What you should not do in any circumstances is to suggest that you have a grievance, even if you are justified, for example, 'After six years of unbroken work for Paterson and Company they have now made me redundant.' Put that way, your prospective employer may well wonder not only why you were picked for redundancy rather than someone else, but may write you off as a trouble maker.

If there are reasons for being made redundant that you would prefer not to mention, your best chance of success lies in diplomatically stressing the advantages of the new job as you see them. You might, therefore, write: 'My present salary is roughly the same as you are offering, but I am attracted by the area in which you operate and by your excellent working conditions.'

When you have made a draft of your letter of application, look at the advertisement carefully once again, and make certain that you have complied with all its requirements. If references are asked for, make sure that you have them, and if five copies are required, send five and not four. If age, current earnings and full Curriculum Vitae are asked for, make sure you include them. The first candidates likely to be eliminated are those who do not conform to the requirements of the advertisement.

There is one exception to this piece of advice. You may feel confident that you could satisfactorily fill a post which you see advertised even though you lack one of the qualifications. It may be that you are a year or two over, or under, the age limits laid down, or that you have been employed for eight instead of ten years, as asked for, at a certain level. It is always possible that the advertiser will not receive anyone with *all* the qualifications they require; it is even possible that they did not expect to, but have asked for so much to attract a high standard of applicant. So if you feel you have a chance, then go ahead; but you should make it clear that you have read the advertisement properly but believe that you have a special case to put forward.

In these circumstances you could end your letter with this brief paragraph: 'In view of my long experience in handling this type of account, and of my varied experience in so many sectors of the computer industry, I feel justified in answering your advertisement even though I am slightly outside the age limits you lay down.'

Finally, there is the all-important overall effect created by your letter. Try to put yourself in the position of the person who will read it. Does it suggest that the writer is lacking in confidence, or that he or she is over-confident? Is there a phrase which suggests too much egocentricity, or another which suggests too much modesty?

References

Employers always ask for references, and it is a good idea to have three or four names ready. Who you choose will depend to some extent on the sort of information they are expected to give about you.

Many employers want information on character rather than qualifications.

Be sure to check if someone is prepared to act as a referee before giving their name.

Dear Mr Tawney,

Now that I have completed my course at the Rodney Technical College I shall be applying for my first job, and I would be most grateful for your help. I think it very likely that I shall be asked to give the name of one or two persons who have known me for a number of years and who could supply a character reference. If I could have permission to give your name I should be very grateful, as you have known our family since you came to the district almost twelve years ago.

Yours sincerely,

If you were asked to provide a reference for someone who had been to the same school as your child, you could answer in one of two ways:

Dear Mrs Sugden,

Thank you for your letter asking for a character reference for .... I have known her for the last ten years. She has always seemed to me to be a person of admirable character, straight-forward, honest and a hard worker.

Yours sincerely,

Alternatively, you might feel that something like the following was needed:

Dear Sir/Madam,

Thank you for asking for a character reference for ..... It is true that I have known her for ten years, but I am afraid that I have not really had a close enough acquaintance with her to be of much use to you.

Yours truly,

In the case of the second letter you had obviously not been forewarned. But what if you *had* been asked, and wanted to refuse for what you felt was a proper reason? In that case you could have replied along the following lines:

Dear Jane,

Thank you for suggesting that you should give my name as a character reference when applying for a job. I would certainly like to help you, but in this case there is a difficulty which I think you will appreciate. This kind of reference should come from someone who has known you far more closely than I have. I am sure you will be able to produce the names of those who will be of far more use to you than I can be.

With best wishes,

When you have secured a job, your employer may well send you a formal letter, but if he does not do so you should confirm the appointment in a letter such as this:

Dear Mr Robson,

Thank you for appointing me your deputy administrator at a salary of £X. a week. I understand that my work will commence on June 1st, and I look forward to meeting you all then.

Yours sincerely,

Letters of resignation

At first sight, it would appear that the task of writing a letter of resignation should offer no difficulties at all. This is far from true. Even if you have already got another job and therefore have no need of a reference now, an employer you have worked for over a period of time could always be a source of one in the future. There is therefore every reason for parting on good terms whatever your personal feelings may be, particularly if your employer suspects that you have been looking for another job. A tactful letter could go something like this:

Dear Mr Wilkinson,

As I think you know, I have for some while been anxious to move to a company where my interest in exports would be given greater scope. In the nature of things it is unlikely that the Wilkinson Company's expansion will be in this direction, and I have now secured a post as export manager of the Guildhome Company.

While I wish to join Guildhome as soon as possible, I do not want to cause you inconvenience. Our formal agreement stipulates a month's notice on either side, but I would be willing to stay on until the rush of the present season's order is over, if this would be helpful. If you could let me know your feelings in the near future I would be most grateful as Guildhome is anxious to know the date I shall be free to join them.

Yours sincerely,

If you are the person receiving the letter of resignation, it is counter-productive to be churlish. Whatever your private feelings, it would be wrong to acknowledge a resignation along the lines of: 'I am surprised that after the long service you have given to this firm you have decided to leave us.' Good employers are not surprised and, in any case, if someone has given long service they should be thanked for it. So why not write this:

Dear Mrs Mackie,

I am sorry to hear that you are leaving us after having given us such good service for so many years. Nevertheless, you have my best wishes in what I hope will be a happy and profitable new job.

Yours sincerely,

Reprimands

While it is the employee who has to use care when writing a letter of resignation, it is the employer who has to exercise judgment when issuing reprimands.

The word 'employer' in this context does not necessarily mean the head of a company. Even if you just have a handful of staff, many of them perhaps working for you only part-time, you may nevertheless find it necessary on occasion to write this sort of letter. Essentially, you must ensure your letter is written without bias or prejudice. Are you relying only on hearsay evidence, which in most cases is decidedly unwise? How serious is the offence? In other words, are you 'making the punishment fit the crime', or are you preparing to write a formal letter of reprimand that will remain on record when a personal word to the person concerned is really all that is needed? And are there any extenuating circumstances, such as illness, domestic anxiety, pressure of work, or the fact that an employee, possibly against his or her own wishes, was standing in for someone else?

It should be remembered that a written reprimand will probably be filed and thus go 'on the record', and if made hastily it could be unfair.

A bad letter would go like this:

Dear Diana,

I have today heard from Messrs Smith and Co that you have not replied to the letter which they sent us a week ago. I have told them that such sloppiness by any member of our staff is most unusual and I have informed them that I will be reprimanding the person concerned. Will you please answer Messrs Smith and Co without delay and see that this lapse is not repeated.

A safer – and fairer – way of writing would be:

Dear Diana,

Smith and Co told me today that they had not yet received a reply to the letter which they wrote to you a week ago. I have assured them that delay in answering correspondence on the part of any member of our firm is most unusual, and have told them that I am asking you to find out what has happened.

If either their letter or a reply from you has gone astray in the post would you please get in touch with them at once. If it has been received, please reply to it without delay, offering your apologies and at the same time let me know what happened.

Yours sincerely,

Dismissals

When dismissing a member of staff, you must take into account the appropriate formal procedures. If the dismissal is judged unfair, then the former employee may be entitled to compensation or even reinstatement.

An unwise letter would read as follows:

Dear Mr Black,

I am hereby giving you the necessary four weeks' notice of termination of engagement, to expire on May 1, after which date your services will no longer be required.

Yours truly,

A safer letter would read:

> Dear Mr Black,
> It is my unpleasant duty to tell you that I am no longer able to employ you and must ask you to accept formal notice from today's date. This step, which I and my colleagues on the board are taking most reluctantly, has been forced on us by the contraction of business. We are all appreciative of everything you have done for us and this will be taken into consideration when we discuss the terms of your severance pay.
> I shall be glad to supply references.
> Perhaps you would telephone my secretary to fix a time when we can meet.
> Yours truly,

In practice, letters of dismissal normally fall somewhere between these two, but there is an essential factor that must be borne in mind. Whatever the circumstances, you should never write anything in a letter of dismissal that could be construed as defamatory. Quite apart from dishonesty, which only the most naive would mention in a letter, there are other aspects which should not be hinted at. Carelessness, inability to get on with other members of the staff, bad time-keeping, and various other failings which, although you might well feel you would be able to substantiate them, should nevertheless be omitted.

Transfers

While a letter of dismissal is one of the most difficult that an employer has to write, an employee can find that being transferred from one place to another presents considerable problems. A letter to your employer written on the following lines might save much heartache:

> Dear Mr Jones,
> Judging by reports in the local papers, the finishing department is to be moved within the next 12 months to Newnham-on-Sea, although some members of staff will be found work in the existing factory.
> I should like to make the strongest possible plea that I should be one such member.

You will see from the records that I have worked in the present factory for 12 years, but this alone is not the main reason for my wish to remain here. I am mid-way through buying my house and while I know that the company is generous in helping to find accommodation and in providing for removal expenses, neither my wife nor myself want to move to a new district so far away. The situation is further complicated by the fact that both of us have elderly relatives nearby.

I am certain you will appreciate our problems and understand that they are causing us considerable anxiety. I would be most grateful to know the position regarding my future employment with the company.

Yours sincerely,

It might be expedient for you to add the following paragraph which would say: 'Although I have always enjoyed working for the company I am afraid I would find it very difficult to remain an employee if this involved moving our home.' You might, of course, write 'impossible' instead of 'very difficult', but this would be distinctly unwise since it is almost the equivalent of giving in your notice.

If this is the first occasion on which the company has been considering a move, you would be justified in asking a number of questions, particularly if you had not made up your mind against the move as definitely as suggested in the above letter. In this case you could say after your opening sentence: 'I myself am not anxious to move and would prefer to remain in the present factory. However, I would be grateful if you could tell me what help will be given to transferred staff in finding new accommodation and in paying for their removal expenses.'

Sales letters

'Sales letters' is a phrase that covers everything from the car salesman's offer of a secondhand Rolls Royce to the duplicated letter pushed through the letterbox. Nevertheless, all such letters have some common factors.

Sales letters often come into the category of junk mail which the recipient tends to put into the waste paper basket without even opening the envelope. Obviously you hope this will not be the case, so make sure that the letter does not contain anything which might reasonably annoy the person receiving it. With some obvious exceptions, the writer of a sales letter is unlikely to know to what political party his potential customer will belong. It is therefore unwise to make any statement which can even indirectly be construed as having political overtones.

Once you have appreciated the pitfalls, it is time to turn to the positive aspects of the sales letter. Here the first point to be made is that a letter which is anything less than completely honest deserves to fail. This applies both to the use of physical description and to wider claims as well. 'In mint condition', 'scarcely used', and 'almost new' are phrases which should be used only if they will stand up to close scrutiny. But it is also inadvisable to say, for instance: 'I sell the world's best and cheapest', while the word 'guarantee' should only be used with care. It would be equally unwise to say: 'I guarantee that you will never regret buying from us', but it would be permissible for you to write: 'I can guarantee that I have been the owner of the car since it was first registered'. In the same way, you can also write: 'I provide a 24-hour service', but you must make sure this is a proper claim.

One possible attention grabber is as follows:

> Dear Occupier,
>
> You are no doubt glad to show your new home to those of your friends and relatives who live near enough to visit it, but what about those who live too far away? A letter on your own headed notepaper is an easy way of telling them where you now live. At the same time it ensures your new address is not misread, which can easily happen.
>
> The cost is by no means high as you will see from the price-list which we enclose.
>
> Yours faithfully,

Alternatively, there are the practical advantages of using your own notepaper which could be stressed like this:

> Dear Occupier,
>
> When you want to write to someone rather special, you may hunt for a sheet of paper and an envelope, and may have to put off writing until the next time the shops are open.

Writing pads can get lost or dirty or even used up for scribbling, but printed notepaper, complete with matching envelopes, is a very different matter.

Printed paper, with its own envelopes, always looks clean and attractive, and takes away the drudgery that sometimes goes with letter-writing.

Whether you are applying for a job, asking for a rise, or just dropping a line to friends you met on holiday, headed notepaper creates a good impression right from the start.

Having your own stationery was once thought of as an extravagance. Nowadays the situation is very different, as you will see from our enclosed list of charges. In fact a trial box of 100 sheets and 50 envelopes will cost you only £X, which is very little compared with some of the items in most weekly budgets.

Yours faithfully,

It is not only in the context of such direct sales that a good letter can make a difference. Those thousands who run small hotels, for instance, can benefit by using tact and imagination in their replies to potential clients.

A typical example could be that of a hotel owner in a popular mountain area. A holiday-maker asking if accommodation was vacant, and enquiring what the cost would be, could well add the following: 'My wife and I are interested in mountain-climbing and also in the possibility of doing some simple scrambling. Could you tell me if there are any instructors in your area?'

Now the person who receives this letter may have come to the area only recently, and may have no special wish to attract ramblers and scramblers. He or she might therefore be tempted to deal with the queries about accommodation and terms, and then add: 'I am afraid that I do not have any information about mountaineering.' This in itself isn't encouraging. Ignorance of what is probably at least a minor local 'industry' suggests the writer might even be unable to help with the local bus timetable. A few enquiries would enable the following more helpful reply to be sent:

Dear ......,

Regarding your enquiry about mountaineering instruction, I am sorry to say that there is none available in the village. However, there is a bus service to the head of the valley and regular daily courses are held there by the .... Group (address), who will be able to help you. In addition, there are four fully qualified guides living not too far away and I understand that all have proved satisfactory to previous visitors to the area. Their names (given in alphabetical order since I am told that all are equally competent) are as follows ...

Yours sincerely,

These are comparatively simple examples of how best to sell your services. It should always be remembered that precautions must be borne in mind when writing this kind of letter. We are not concerned here with cases of dishonesty, or of a firm taking deliberate advantage of customers. This is increasingly covered by the law. Far more important are the genuine misunderstandings which can arise from ambiguity.

The most obvious problem could be date of delivery. A confectioner might, for instance, be ordering four hundred Easter eggs. But the order should stipulate that they must be delivered by mid-February. Otherwise, the confectioner might be forced to pay for them even if they arrived only a few days before Easter.

In much buying and selling no formal contract is exchanged, and in such cases it is the final written acceptance of an offer which in effect becomes the contract.

This means that acceptance should contain the delivery date and anything else which is relevant, including any details that have only been agreed verbally. If the full details of the transaction have been outlined in previous correspondence it would be possible to simplify matters by saying that the contract is subject to the conditions which you set down in your letter of a specific date.

You may wonder why it is necessary to set down in writing details that you have agreed with someone you can trust. The point at issue is not one of honesty but of common sense. If some disagreement arises in the future the person with whom you deal could have died, or could have left the firm. It is always sensible to take precautions. Even if you are conducting business with a friend or relative there is no reason for not being clear-cut.

One all too frequent cause of misunderstanding is lack of clarity, for example, whether a letter in reply to an offer is an acceptance or merely a show of interest. Suppose, for instance, that an office equipment firm, knowing that you are interested in certain items, has sent you a letter saying:

> Dear Mr Slade,
> In connection with your recent enquiry we can offer you a good, reconditioned Panasonic fax/answerphone model … at £X; a new but shop-soiled Hewlett Packard bubble jet printer model ... at £X; and an overhauled Xerox copier model … at £X
> Yours sincerely,

If, after considering the offer, you feel that you are merely a potential buyer, you could reply as follows:

> Dear Mr Owen,
> Thank you for your offer of office equipment detailed in your letter of December 1st. I am interested, but before ordering any of these items would wish to try them out in our Broad Street office. Would it be possible for you to let me have any, or all of them, for a one- or two-day trial?
> Yours truly,

If you feel that the prices are high, you could well say so and ask: 'If all three were bought together would it be possible for you to offer a discount?' Either letter will make it clear that you are not ordering the equipment.

If, however, you have decided that you do want to purchase, there will be little point in replying: 'Thank you for your offer of the three items listed in your letter of December 1st. It seems that they will meet our requirements, and the prices seem to be about right. I would be grateful if you could let me know about delivery.'

The receiver of such a letter could well assume that you had ordered the three items. However, you do not say so in so many words, while the final sentence suggests that your acceptance might be conditional on delivery being by a specific date. In these circumstances you might find the goods had been sold to someone else.

This could be avoided if you replied as follows:

> Dear Mr Owen,
>
> Thank you for your letter of December 1st offering us a reconditioned Panasonic fax/ answerphone model ... at £X; a new but shop-soiled Hewlett Packard bubble jet printer model ... at £X; and an overhauled Xerox copier model … at £X
>
> We accept your offer and would be glad if you would deliver the three machines as soon as possible. We must make our acceptance conditional on the machines being delivered within four weeks, but I imagine there is no problem with this.
>
> Yours sincerely,

You will note that you have not only listed the three items but have repeated the firm's 'good, reconditioned' and 'new but shop-soiled'. There can, of course, always be argument about how good is 'good' but you have given yourself some protection if any of the equipment turns out to be unsatisfactory.

You will, in any case, almost certainly be protected to some extent by recent consumer legislation although there are, of course, two self-protecting steps which you should take as a matter of course: inspect the equipment personally before entering into any negotiations and deal only with a firm which is well established and has a reputation for fair dealing.

Most problems arise from genuine misunderstandings and this is particularly true when the matter involves not a physical object, such as a piece of office equipment, but a mixture of service and accommodation. All too often one can get caught up in embarrassing circumstances that could have been avoided by giving a little additional thought to the letters written. Typical of many a misunderstanding was that of a firm whose proprietor was building up a successful business in hand-made jewellery. He heard that a nearby town was preparing to hold an Industry Fair and thought it would be beneficial if he took a stand and exhibited. All he needed to say in writing to the organizer was something like this:

Dear Organizer,

I should be grateful if you would send me details of the Industry Fair which you are organizing in Extown later this year, including the costs of hiring a display stand.

Yours faithfully,

Instead, what he wrote was this: 'I have heard that you are organising an Industry Fair in Extown later this year. I think that it would be a good place for me to display examples of the hand-made jewellery which is made in my workshop here, and I would like to do this. Please send particulars – I hope it is not too late to book a stand, as I know that this sometimes has to be arranged a very long time in advance.'

This was a bad letter because it failed to put across one important fact: that the letter-writer was merely a potential exhibitor and wanted to know how much a site in the Fair would cost. It is true that in a court of law his letter might not be considered as a contract to take space, even though many hotel owners receive letters from clients who expect a room to be reserved for them on the strength of nothing more definite.

However, the jewellery-maker was shocked to receive a letter which said:

Dear Sir,

Thank you for your letter of January 4th. As you thought, space begins to book up more than a year ahead and all the space had been booked when I received your letter. However, this morning's post brought a cancellation and I have therefore reserved for you one of our standard display areas, six foot by eight feet at the standard rate of £X per square foot. The fee of £X is payable at once and I shall be glad to receive your cheque together with any further instructions which can be carried out in accordance with the enclosed schedule of charges.

Yours faithfully,

The only places where the craftsman had previously exhibited his jewellery had been at small village events and he had not expected space at the Industry Fair to be so expensive. But he now compounded his mistake by doing nothing until he had a reminder for the fee in a letter which said that the date for cancellation was past. He then wrote the following: 'I am sorry that I have not replied earlier to your first letter. I was honestly surprised to get your second letter this morning since when I wrote I was really only making a general enquiry about taking space. I did not realize that the charges would be as high as they are, and it would never be worth my while to display my goods in this way. I do hope that you will therefore agree to my cancelling my order as a small business like mine could never stand the expense.'

This was a poor letter in its phrasing and a worse one in that it specifically spoke of 'cancelling' and 'order'. The organizer of the Fair had been doing his job as a salesperson and trying to turn a potential buyer into a real one, but until the use of the word 'order' he would have had little chance of making an issue out of it.

In the circumstances, the jeweller should have responded to the first letter in terms such as these:

> Dear Sir,
>
> Thank you for sending me particulars of the Industry Fair which I asked for in my letter of January 4th. I have, however, decided against taking space at this event.
>
> Yours truly,

Alternatively, he could, as a precaution, have gone to his solicitor who could have sent a letter to the organizer discouraging him from making any formal attempt to secure payment in such a poor case. The letter to the solicitor, which should have been accompanied by a copy of the original letter to the organizer and a copy of the reply, should have gone like this:

> Dear Mr Black,
>
> I recently enquired about taking space at the Industry Fair to be held later this year and have received a reply from the organizer who has mistakenly taken my letter as an order. I am enclosing a copy of my letter and a copy of his. I should be grateful if you would write to him pointing out that I have not placed an order. I will telephone you about this within the next two days.
>
> Yours sincerely,

The point about telephoning is that if the solicitor has any minor points that he wishes to raise they can probably be settled more quickly – and more cheaply – by a few words on the telephone than by an exchange of letters.

Overdue payments, orders, etc.

Retrieving yourself from a situation in which you have made a mistake can call for a careful mixture of tact and firmness. The same is true when you are demanding money in settlement of an unpaid account.

The situation will be governed by your own judgment on whether lack of payment is due to an oversight, an attempt to avoid payment, or an inability to pay. You are unlikely to be sure of the answer and it is important to send a first letter along the following lines:

> Dear Sir/Madam,
>
> We note that our account for £3,000 dated May 4th, 2003, has not yet been settled. As you know, our conditions of sale include payment one month from invoicing, and I imagine that the delay has occurred owing to the present busy state of the trade.
>
> Nevertheless, it is now seven weeks since date of invoicing and we would much appreciate settlement.
>
> Yours faithfully,

If this fails to produce payment within a week a sterner note is called for;

> Dear Sir/Madam,
>
> We have still not received settlement of our account for £3,000 dated May 4th, 2003, and must now ask for a cheque without further delay.
>
> Yours truly,

If no payment follows promptly it would be a good idea to take the next step:

Dear Sir/Madam,

Having received no acknowledgement of our letters of June 24th and July 1st, and no settlement of our account for £3,000 dated May 4th, 2003, we shall be forced to put the matter in the hands of our solicitors if payment is not made by return.

Yours truly,

The same policy of 'hurrying slowly' is usually the best to adopt when writing business letters of complaint, whether the trouble is bad workmanship or non-delivery. In the case of the latter it is always wise to realize that the fault may not lie with the supplier. He or she may, in fact, be just as perturbed as the non-receiver who will gain little from adopting the 'unless' attitude. It is bad policy, for instance, to write: 'Only six of the dozen photographic enlargers ordered last May have so far arrived. We are now running up to the post-holiday period when we have our biggest demand, and unless the missing six arrive within the next fortnight I shall refuse to accept them.' Before putting your complaint on paper it is essential to look at your order and at the supplier's note of acceptance. You may then find that you cannot, in any case, 'refuse to accept'; alternatively, you may find that you *can* refuse. But in neither case would the above letter be a good one. If there is nothing in the order stipulating date of delivery, the following letter should be written:

Dear Mr Black,

Six of the dozen photographic enlargers which we ordered from you last May have not yet been delivered. I am certain you will appreciate that the post-holiday months which will soon be with us are by far the best for sales of enlargers. We are hoping to encourage these in this area and trust you will do everything possible to ensure that we do not run out of stock at this time of the year.

Yours truly,

Even if there is a stipulation in the order that the goods must arrive by a certain time, an unnecessary cancellation will do little to ensure adequate service in the future. In these circumstances you should write as follows:

Dear Mr Black,
We have still not received six of the photographic enlargers ordered from you last May. As you will see from the order the final date for delivery is only a week away. Your firm is no doubt as anxious as we are to ensure that this equipment is put on the market this month when some of the holidays are already over and circumstances are so good for sales. Can you please let us know without delay whether we are to receive the enlargers by the agreed date?
Yours truly,

The answer to this last letter might, if you were unlucky, be along the following lines:

Dear Mr Johnson,
Thank you for your letter of ... dealing with delivery of enlargers. I am sorry to say that the manufacturers have had production problems, and it seems likely that we shall be getting only about three-quarters of our promised supplies.

As wholesalers we are as anxious to supply the goods as you are to sell them, but will understand your position if you feel it necessary to cancel the order for the outstanding items. Can I suggest that you wait until the end of the month and that we review the situation then.

Meanwhile, we will put all possible pressure on the manufacturers.
Yours sincerely,

In such a situation you might feel it necessary to hold a meeting with your sales staff and, afterwards, to write a brief account on what had taken place. The need for a concise record, less formal than a fully-blown report but nevertheless describing a meeting in some detail, is by no means confined to those in 'big business'. Even if your firm is only a small one it will be useful to have on record an objective account of what happened.

If you are writing a report to a partner or to a superior, this can form part of the body of the letter, but it is usually better to write it out separately and refer to it in the letter.

Reporting meetings

To take a rather more important example than the one just dealt with, you might consider the situation arising out of a discussion about the site of new premises. If it was your job to report on the meeting, refer to it briefly in the accompanying letter which should say: 'John Brown came to discuss the site of the new premises and I am enclosing an account of the meeting.'

The account should be strictly objective. In other words you should not allow your own opinions to become mixed up with what Mr Brown reported – although you can of course put your views at the end of the report.

You should also remember that the account may be passed on to others who do not have as much background knowledge as you have. Because of this, the report should be self-contained and should include all the relevant information. Above all, avoid woolly statements like this: 'Mr Brown came to discuss his views on where the new premises should be sited, and although he brought his labour expert with him I was not much impressed by what he had to say. His accountant whom he also brought along with him may be right about the Government support we might obtain, but I really think that other factors, which I pointed out in our discussion, are far more important. I am also against going into Linkthorpe, even though most of the other possibilities were ruled out.'

Instead, head the sheet of paper like this:

Report of a meeting held in the offices of
Camdex Ltd, Burt Road, Cheswall
on March 9, 2003,
to discuss the best site for the proposed
new assembly works

Present John Brown, chief technical consultant, Brown & Cranford, architects
Elaine Wright, chief accountant, Brown & Cranford
Anthony Pringle, labour manager, Brown & Cranford
Ronald Tucker, deputy chairman, Camdex Ltd (writer)

After this, the report could continue as follows:

'Mr Brown said that as instructed he had made a survey of possible sites for the new assembly works within ten miles of the main factory. Two – those at Crumbley and Overstall – had been quickly ruled out, since it was discovered that the freeholders were not prepared to lease on realistic terms, or to sell.

A possible site at Hambleford was in many ways ideal, but the area has poor communications. Although, as Mr Brown pointed out, it would be possible for us to provide buses for the small number of staff who would be involved, he felt that the isolation of the area would make it difficult to attract workers. Mr Pringle felt even more strongly that this would be the case.

Two sites at Maggotsford and Brandon were ruled out when Mr Brown reported that local building restrictions would prevent us from erecting buildings to our specifications.

Mr Brown then went on to say that he had investigated the sixth site, at Linkthorpe, and considered that this was the best available. Mr Pringle commented that while labour was scarce in this area, he thought that Camdex had a good enough reputation to attract the comparatively small numbers that would be required. Ms Wright supported Mr Brown on the grounds that Linkthorpe lies just within one of the local development areas, and thought it possible that Government support might be obtained.

My own view is that the Linkthorpe site would have disadvantages as great as that at Hambleford. Labour of the right quality has been a problem on previous occasions, and I suggest that before going ahead we should make another effort to find a more suitable site. Before this is done, the possibility of going slightly further afield might be investigated. Perhaps Mr Durley, our transport manager, could give us a brief note on increased costs, etc., if the new unit was twelve or fifteen miles away.'

Writing abroad

Letters to holiday friends you have met abroad should present no particular problems, and the same is obviously true of correspondence with in-laws or other relatives who are not of your own nationality. Business letters are a totally different matter.

First you have to take a decision on whether you should write in English or in the language of the country you are writing to. There are some countries in which letters written in English are perfectly acceptable. India, for instance, which has a large number of local languages and dialects, is a case in point; the same is true of many Middle Eastern countries. In Scandinavia a letter in English will almost always be understood, although one written in the recipient's own language is likely to give the writer an advantage over competitors who omit this courtesy. Elsewhere, however, and certainly in most of the EU countries, as well as in others in Europe, a letter in the language of the person to whom you are writing is helpful.

If you are fluent in the language of your correspondent, you will have no problem. For those who are not linguists there are two alternatives. The first is to draft your letter in English and have it translated. Most towns have efficient translation agencies, and while their fees may at first seem high the money is invariably well spent. The alternative is to write in English as it is important to avoid attempting to use a language with which you cannot cope. The wrong use of a word or phrase can easily lead to misunderstandings, and even to legal difficulties if you have intended to say one thing and have in fact said another. Basically, it is a good policy to get your letter competently translated. Ignorance never inspires confidence.

Europe

Before writing to a client in Europe you should have made yourself familiar with some of the ways in which the client's background life is different from your own. Public holidays, for instance, are different world-wide, and business hours could start earlier or end later. Also don't forget the time differences between countries.

Remember, also, that every country has its own conventions regarding modes of address. In France 'Monsieur' is used even before 'President' which means both Chairman and President. Europeans tend to be rather particular about formalities, and a little trouble taken in getting these right will pay dividends. Most Embassies, however, have an official whose task it is to straighten out the more obvious problems that the small businessman has to face. Many countries have separate import-export or trading groups, and the fullest use should be made of them, particularly before negotiations are opened for the first time.

Every country has its own traditions and conventions as to the way that business is done. Accepting these is the sort of courtesy which oils the wheels of trade.

The Middle East

While the need to brief yourself properly on conditions abroad is necessary when dealing with European countries, it is even more important when writing to the Middle East. Here, convention, climate – and, not least, religion – are all so very different from those in the USA, Britain and Europe.

However, this is the general advice given by an expert with long experience of trading in this area:

- Remember that any sign of brusqueness can be interpreted as lack of interest. A sense of proportion is obviously called for, but what might sound rather extravagant in a letter to a foreign firm could be correct in Middle Eastern terms.
- Unless you know your correspondent very well indeed, avoid personal enquiries or expressions of interest in family affairs.
- When you receive a letter from a Middle Eastern correspondent, make certainly that your reply is sent off as quickly as possible. Businessmen in this area prefer to carry out their business by means of personal contact rather than by correspondence, and a letter sent out is an indication of enthusiasm. Maintain this enthusiasm by sending a prompt reply.

North America

When writing to clients in the USA, it is worth remembering that although the British, Americans and Canadians all speak the same language, there are many colloquial differences.

Some words have one meaning in Britain and another in North America; the US meaning for a word may even be the reverse of the British meaning. A case in point is the word billion. In Britain it means one million million (1,000,000,000,000 – frequently written 1,000,000M), while in the United States it means one thousand million (1,000,000,000 or 1,000M). As an example of a word meaning one thing in Britain and its reverse in the United States, take is the verb 'to table'. In Britain, 'tabling' a motion means that it is set down for discussion; in the United States it means that the motion is set aside rather than discussed.

In addition to the words and phrases that are likely to crop up in business correspondence there are others that can easily cause confusion. Thus in Britain a 'public school' is a fee-paying – in fact a non-public – school, whereas in the United States the phrase has the more straightforward meaning of a school used by the public, in other words a state school.

Now it is obviously impossible for the writer to be aware of all these pitfalls – but there are in existence inexpensive English-American dictionaries. Anyone likely to be writing to the United States regularly would be well advised to invest in one of these. Failing this, however, try to show a draft of your opening correspondence to someone who is likely to spot any obvious errors.

Another point which should be remembered when writing to the United States is not merely the size of the country but the differences in outlook between one part and another. The flourishing, and more conservative, cities of the Eastern seaboard are not only as far from California as London is from Beirut, but their outlooks are almost as different.

Remember that the United States has no 'national' daily newspapers in the British sense of the phrase. East coast and West coast are separated not only by the Rocky Mountains but by the thousands of miles of rolling prairies making up the Middle West. So if you are doing business with someone in San Francisco, the fact that you have already been successful in Boston will not necessarily help, and may even be a handicap since local conditions can be completely different.

Here is the wrong way of going about writing to Mr Cyrus Rockefeller, president of a large printing agency in San Francisco:

> Dear Sir/Madam,
>
> As the manufacturers of a unique form of photographic printing equipment which has been successfully on sale throughout the Continent of Europe for more than 20 years, we are anxious to sell our products in North America and would like to know whether you would consider handling this equipment.
>
> Our firm has been in existence since 1820, and our products have brought tributes from satisfied users in many Continental countries.

I enclose a printed prospectus giving details of the equipment and would be glad to have this demonstrated to you should you be visiting the United Kingdom. I myself may be visiting the United States later this year and would be glad to discuss details with you in New York.

Yours sincerely,

To start at the beginning, the 'Dear Sir/Madam' should be 'Dear Mr Rockefeller' or even 'Dear President'. Next, 'unique' is a very dangerous word to use unless you are completely up to date with the latest developments in the United States. In addition, the fact that your equipment has been successfully in use for more than 20 years could easily produce the reaction: 'What, 20 years old! Surely there must be something better by now.' Then the phrase 'North America'. This includes Canada as well as the United States and Mexico, countries with different laws, traditions and, in many ways, requirements. The fact that your firm has been in existence for more than a century and a half is not necessarily a recommendation. The suggestion in the last paragraph that your potential customer should go out of his way on your account would be bad enough in any letter; here it is compounded by the idea that he might be willing to make a trip of some 2,500 miles just to see you.

The following would have a far greater chance of success:

Dear Mr Rockefeller,

The latest model of our photographic printing equipment with its quick production of immaculate results is particularly suited to the demands of a richly developing state such as California. We have been searching for a forward-looking group which would be able to handle its sale and believe that yours might be the ideal corporation to do this.

I enclose with this letter our latest brochure giving details of what this remarkable equipment can do and a list of the terms on which we have successfully extended its use in other countries.

Although we are about to market the latest models in other countries, we have not as yet approached the United States. I shall, of course, be delighted to arrange a demonstration for you in San Francisco so that you can assess the value of the equipment for yourself.

If there are any further details which you would like to have, I will ensure that you receive these without delay.

Sincerely,

In other words, be friendly, offer service, and have no inhibitions about praising your own goods. That advice should be followed in virtually every business letter you are ever likely to write abroad.

Setting up abroad

Even the comparatively small business person may have contacts with foreign countries that involve more than buying and selling. He or she may, for instance, wish to set up in business abroad, having first checked, of course, that there are no impediments as far as any regulations are concerned. In this case it is absolutely essential to gather as much information as possible before making any plans. The first step would be to write a brief letter to the commercial attaché's department, which could go along these lines:

Dear Sir/Madam,

I am anxious to set up a small assembly works near the town of ... and would be grateful if you would let me know to whom I should send particulars of my proposals.

Yours faithfully,

The answer will of course depend on the country. The likelihood is that you will be advised to write first to a department of the country's central government, although in some cases you may be referred to a regional authority. In either case, you should ask a number of relevant questions.

Dear Sir/Madam,

I am contemplating an extension of my business as manufacturer of specialised do-it-yourself equipment into ... The Trade Counsellor at your Embassy has suggested that I should get in touch with you and I shall be very grateful for any help which you can give me.

I founded ... at the above address in ... and our turnover has steadily built up to its present figure of £X per annum. Many items in our range are in great demand in your country and I have for some while been considering setting up a small factory for their assembly, employing between 40 and 50 local people in the ... area.

I would therefore much appreciate it if you could answer the following questions:

1 What permission is required from local or other authorities for the setting-up of such a factory?
2 What is the current availability of labour in this area and the regulations governing employment?
3 While about 50 per cent of our materials could be bought locally, we would need to import a number of components (listed on a separate enclosed sheet) for assembly in the new factory, at least until provision was made for their manufacture locally. I would like to know what import duties would be imposed in these circumstances.
4 I would wish to employ three or four administrators, at least for the first year of the factory's operation, and would be glad to know whether work permits would be granted for them.
5 Are there at present in force any specific laws which you feel might affect the successful running of such an assembly works?

I shall, of course, be glad to visit you to discuss the matter in detail at any mutually convenient time.

Yours faithfully,

Filling in forms

While more letters are probably being written now than ever before, the number of forms which have to be filled in is also increasing. The average person will probably have to fill in forms for a television licence, a driving licence, a car licence, a children's allowance, and even the mailing of a packet overseas, and there are certain common sense rules to be observed with all of them.

The first is to read the form carefully from beginning to end before you begin to fill it in. When you start to do that, remember that most forms should be completed either in black biro or on a typewriter, except for the signature which must be handwritten. Pencil is not good enough. Start at the beginning and work your way through to the end, remembering that there are probably places or boxes where you have to put a tick or cross. Do not leave any questions to be filled in later or you may forget to do them and send the form off incomplete.

Many forms also include alternative phrases or even alternative sentences which, leaving the appropriate ones, have to be scored through. These may vary from: 'I am/am not over 21' to 'Please credit the proceeds to my account No ... at ... Branch of ... Bank/Please send me a cheque for the proceeds'. If you fail to do the necessary crossing-out, the form will come back.

There are other cases – notably the forms which have to be filled in for Value Added Tax – where the answer is 'None', and the word 'None' must be written in, a simple dash being insufficient.

Overall, the most important thing with form-filling is to take the greatest pains to be absolutely accurate in the answers that you make to any questions. Failure to give the correct answer can, for instance, invalidate an insurance policy or lead to considerable trouble if money is involved in the payment of pensions or allowances.

5 communicating with the media

In this chapter you will learn:

- **how to communicate with the media – with newspapers and magazines, television and radio**
- **about letters to agony aunts and their replies.**

Now that we have such a sophisticated world media, the right kind of communication is essential.

Letters to newspapers

You may wish to make public a complaint or some grievance against the authorities; you may wish to ask for information; you may wish to air your opinions – which other people can of course always call your prejudices! – on some matter in which you are a specialist; you may wish to state your views on a subject of public importance which is being nationally debated. Whatever your reason for writing to the editor, two important points must be remembered.

The first is that every newspaper in the country receives far more letters than it can print. With the best will in the world, those chosen are a selection and there is no justification for feeling enraged if yours is not among them.

The second point is that virtually all editors reserve the right to shorten letters before they are printed. Without the existence of this proviso they would be forced to print even fewer letters than they do now.

When shortening letters a newspaper should, of course, alter neither its sense nor its balance. Whether or not this is done can be a matter of opinion, and it is easy for a writer who has carefully balanced half a dozen points to feel that that balance has been altered. If this happens, ask the opinion of someone who is not personally involved – with you, with the paper, or with the argument. If the verdict, after reading your original letter – and the form in which it was printed – is that a distortion has been made, a further letter may help.

Dear Editor,

In printing my letter on divorce on May 24 I notice that you omitted the fourth paragraph. I appreciate that some shortening of letters is often necessary, and that in this case the point left out may at first sight appear to be a minor one. However, in the opinion of those who have studied the subject deeply the qualification I made is in fact of considerable importance, and I should be grateful if you would make it clear that after dealing with the question of custody I wrote ...'

Yours truly,

You may not be lucky. But if you fail with this kind of letter you are pretty certain to fail with any other. You can, of course, complain to the Press Council, but it would be advisable to do this only if the incident has involved an obvious distortion.

How do you begin a letter to the Editor? In many cases you start by being assertive. If you wish to add to the debate about the training of mountaineers it will help if you can establish that you are speaking from experience: 'As a member of two Everest expeditions, and with experience of Alpine climbing during ten seasons ...' If you start your letter by saying: 'As a member of the Little Morton Lawn Tennis Club I feel qualified to offer some advice about the current Wimbledon controversy', it will not carry much weight.

You should remember that even in correspondence with relatively small local papers, your letter is likely to be scrutinized by a number of genuine experts. If it is printed in a national newspaper you may have some of the best brains in the country trying to pick holes in it.

This is no reason for timidity, or for failing to write, but it is a reason for going over your letter when it has been written and checking every detail. If you are wrong on even a minor point you will have opened the way for the experts to cast doubt on more than this small error: 'I notice that Mr James fails to give even the correct date on which the first contribution to the controversy was made, and I am therefore wondering what reliance can be put on any of his more complicated and important figures.' So take extra precautions to get even the smallest fact correct.

Another point to watch if your letter deals, for instance, with complaints about local affairs, is the use of dangerous over-generalizations. After discussions with your neighbours, you may be tempted to start a letter with the words: 'Everyone in Larkspur Road agrees that the proposed construction of a new club at the bottom of the street is most unwelcome and will, if carried out, lower both the tone of the street and the value of the houses in it.' Now it is extremely unlikely that such a statement would be true; and even if it were you would probably have some difficulty in substantiating the facts. 'Everyone' means everyone. What you really mean is that a large number of friends and acquaintances agree with you.

There is no escape from the word 'everyone', as you will see from this letter: 'Mr Smith is completely wrong in claiming that everyone in Larkspur Road objects to the proposed new club.

I regard it as an additional amenity and believe that there are many other residents who think as I do. I hope that if any protest is being planned – which I personally would much regret – it will at least be organized on sensible grounds and not open itself up to ridicule with the exaggerated claims that often make protest movements look more ludicrous than rational.' In such a case, the one enthusiastic word 'everyone' would have done the cause little good.

Letters to the newspapers are often used to arouse interest in the commemoration of local people or events. The choice usually has to be made between a letter so long that it will probably be drastically cut or another which fails to provide enough detail. It is sometimes possible to avoid this difficulty by first writing to the editor a letter which is not intended for publication. It could go something like this:

Dear Sir/Madam,

As you no doubt know, next year marks the centenary of the birth in Hamchester of the architect Sir James Gilmore who not only designed many of the most important buildings in the town but who has achieved some fame for his other works throughout the country. I and a number of interested friends want to commemorate Sir James's birth, possibly by a public exhibition in the town, and I am wondering whether you would be willing to give publicity to such proposals. I would be glad to outline what we have in mind, and would be grateful to know the length of any letter to which you would be able to give space.

Yours faithfully,

Such a letter might very well produce a call from one of the paper's reporters and this would enable you to outline your plans in detail. At the very worst you might get a reply saying that, due to pressure on space, your letter should be kept down to 200 words or so. However, all that you really have to say at this stage is this: 'Next year will see the centenary of the birth in Hamchester of the well-known architect, Sir James Gilmore who died in ... I am hoping to organize an exhibition to commemorate the event and would be glad if anyone who might be able to help would get in touch with me at the above address.'

In a case like this you could write similar letters to the specialist journals of the architectural press. You might know their titles, but if not you can consult the various press directories in the library.

In any letter to the press you should take particular care about libel. All newspapers have a lawyer who reads proofs in an effort to ensure that nothing libellous is actually printed. Nevertheless, the number of libel cases which reach the courts – only a percentage of those which are settled outside – is an indication that lawyers are not infallible.

There is one special point to be watched here. You might, for instance, write in all innocence: 'There is really no reason why the views about the safety of the new electric grid expressed in your issue of June 4 by James Todd should be taken more seriously than those of anyone else.' The newspaper might not suspect that there was anything dangerous in this opinion, but if Mr Todd was a senior electrical consultant the position would be rather different; and if he could show that an important item of professional work had not gone his way because of your letter, he would be in a strong position to sue.

As a final point, be prepared for the fact that a single, brief letter in a local paper could involve you in a lengthy correspondence. You have been warned!

Media standards

Complaining about or praising standards of television, radio, newspapers and magazines should always be aired immediately. Some major TV networks carry such letters and some programmes on radio have a post bag.

The human condition dictates that complaints are far more regular than praise, but let's be encouraging and start with the praise. The letters should always be brief and to the point, such as the following:

Dear Producer,

I was most impressed by the objective reporting in your recent programme on fox hunting. You showed both sides of the controversy very clearly and did not become involved with either side. What a refreshing change.

Yours sincerely,

Of course if you were a farmer, a hunter or a protestor you would be even more qualified to praise the programme's objectivity – provided that you were able to distance yourself from the problem too.
But if you are going to complain, then don't sound subjective and hysterical, bigoted or enraged – even if you are! The cool, logical approach is inevitably the one favoured for transmission unless, of course, you are prepared to risk being a wild eccentric who can be publicly mocked.

This is probably what would happen, if you wrote the following:

Dear Producer,

All I can say about fox hunters – and any other kind of hunter – is that they are an unspeakable blot on our moral landscape and should be publicly executed.

Your programme clearly took their side at all times and I feel the same punishment should be meted out to you as well.

Yours sincerely,

By remaining more objective, you will have far better results:

Dear Producer,

I was most concerned about your programme 'Widening the Gap' which was so heavily biased towards those who hunt. Obviously their point of view must be recorded but surely, so should that of the anti-hunting lobby.

By concentrating on filming the rally, you simply made them the object of abuse and there was no chance for them to put their case.

Yours sincerely,

Agony Aunts

The agony aunts of the media, rather like dating agencies, have recently become much more professional and the derision that they formerly attracted has lessened.

I reproduce one such letter and some responses, all of which employ an excellent economy of style.

The problem

My sister-in-law, who is now in her late seventies and in poor health, is a very religious Jewess. Her younger son, who lives in another country, some years ago married a non-Jewish girl. The news was kept from her by her husband, who has a more conventionally Orthodox background. It was obviously impossible for this situation to continue indefinitely and earlier this year he told his wife. Despite her unhappiness, she has since then refused to speak to her son and dislikes to hear his name mentioned. While she has not gone into ceremonial mourning for him, as strict Orthodox practice requires for one who has 'married out', she has cut him off entirely. I am enough of an Orthodox Jew to sympathize with her. Others are outspoken in their criticism of what they consider her fanatic subordination of personal relationships to outworn religious belief. So, what is to be done? Does one denounce the son? Praise the mother for her adherence to religious principle? Or regard her as a silly, inflexible old woman? Is there any compromise?

The responses

I cannot believe a loving God would have any sympathy with this woman. She should be persuaded to see a Rabbi of enlightened views who will help her to realize that she will receive great blessings if contact with her son and her new daughter-in-law is resumed.

Ann Walden, High Wycombe

The trouble with our religion is that for it to survive, it can't be altered. If you keep diluting the same glass of orange squash, you will end up with pure water. For us to be members of a club, we must abide by its rules. Judaism is not in essence a religion, but a way of life.

For most of my life, I rejected the religion because I could not come to terms with so many of its aspects that didn't make sense or have any apparent reason. I also believed that people would judge me and say: 'Well, if you don't keep this law, then why keep that one?' Six years ago, something happened to cause me to return. I now keep what I like when I like. I don't take any notice of any criticism from any mortal being. The only entity that may judge us is the Almighty.

Your sister-in-law is wrong to cut off her son. He was obviously 'lost' to her many years ago. It is far better that he has found happiness with someone whom he loves and who loves him, than that he be miserably married to a Jewish girl.

Name and address withheld

As an Indian Hindu woman going out with an Englishman, I sympathize with the predicament of a family divided by love and religion. It is difficult to convince parents that your choice of partner is not a selfish, whimsical decision. It is certainly the biggest decision I've had to make in my life.

When I first decided to tell my parents about my boyfriend, I steadfastly and stubbornly believed that it was the rest of the world who was unfair, intolerant and inflexible. It was a shock for me to discover that the simplified 'us and them' of mixed marriages is a myth. Despite their outrage and opposition, my parents proved to be decent, kind and rational people whose only concern was for the future well-being of their daughter. Their concerns are no different from those of most parents: to want the very best for their children. As a family from an ethnic background already holding on to its roots by a thread, the wish extends to the continued practice of my religion, my language and my culture, and to instil the long-held beliefs in my future children.

My advice to the son would be to grit his teeth and make contact with his mother. He will have to do all the work because, in her eyes, he has betrayed her and the faith. The mother will never approve of him, but one day she may learn to accept him and his wife. If my parents had cut themselves off from me, they would have engineered the very thing they feared: the loss of contact with my culture and religion.

I may never gain approval of the route I have taken. I will not, however, skulk away and live my life in shame, away from my community. I will continue to bring my boyfriend to my home until he is accepted as the man I choose to be with. This is not through spiteful obstinacy, but the only way forward. Everyone has had a chance to shout, cry and berate each other. Now my boyfriend feels less alienated by getting a glimpse of the traditions of my culture and my parents see him as an individual who just might make their daughter happy.

Name and address withheld

The problem has been expressed from the viewpoint of Jewish orthodoxy, yet the deeper emotion here seems to be one of simple, old-fashioned control: the mother considering her son as personal property. Maybe the primary error was not to inform her of the marriage when it occurred because such conspiracy suggests that the aggrieved party has power, which is not really the case. The woman is approaching 80 and the thought of conversion is naive. The more anxious relatives seek to placate, creating the 'confirmation' that in some strange way she has indeed been aggrieved.

I have had to go through this agonizing break myself and, at the age of 35, had to state clearly to my mother that I was my own person and intended to remain that way. We never spoke again and she died two years later.

It is interesting that many sons – perhaps daughters too – are forced to emigrate to deal with this hideous problem of maternal control in a different way. Whatever method is used, please do not use endless placation as it becomes very enjoyable to self-made martyrs.

Name and address withheld

Raised as a liberal Jew, who then 'married out' but was not cast out by my family, I admit that it is hard for me to sympathize with, let alone praise, your sister-in-law's attitude. But she holds it sincerely and right now all one can do is accept and try to respect this.

Sadly, it is not in the son's power to effect a reconciliation. Only your sister-in-law could do that: is there a glimmer of hope in the fact that she stopped short of the full mourning ritual? If he has not already done so, the errant son could write, just once, to his mother, express his great sadness that she has cut him off in this way and his sincere hope that somehow, some day, they may speak again.

Meanwhile, you, in that uncomfortable piggy-in-the-middle position, can perhaps try to leave a door open. Is it possible to talk about the situation with her in terms of the personal pain her son has caused her, rather than the ultimate 'wrong' she believes him to have done? If so, maybe something just might ease up before she dies.

Helen Gamsa, Bristol

Writing to the media is your right and must be exercised. If you remember the advice given in this chapter you stand a far greater chance of being heard.

06 the internet and e-mail

In this chapter you will learn:

- **how to communicate via e-mail – to individuals and to groups of people.**

The Internet is a global network that electronically links millions of individuals and businesses, people and organizations, who communicate with each other through their computers.

All that is required to join the Internet is a computer, a modem, suitable software, a communications link (such as your existing telephone line) and an account with an Internet Service Provider.

The facilities can get the individual on-line anywhere in the world for the price of a local telephone call, and provide an extraordinary number of services, ranging from the resources of libraries and universities to shopping malls and computer games to personal chat lines, news groups and much else.

If you want to know more about the Internet and getting on-line, you might like to read *Teach Yourself The Internet*. Our focus here is on e-mail and its relationship to letter-writing.

One of the most widely used Internet services is e-mail (electronic mail). Using e-mail, it is possible to send and receive text messages or computer files of information to and from anywhere in the world. Any message that is sent to your e-mail address will be held in your Service Provider's mail server (computer) until you log-in and download it. Security is provided for your personal e-mail, because it can only be accessed with your own log-in name and password.

If very high security is needed, messages can be sent using a special encryption system, such that it can only be decoded by someone who knows the necessary keyword.

E-mail is also present on most office networks, where it can play an important part in the organization's internal communications.

There are some distinct advantages to e-mail:

- speed – sometimes mail is delivered almost immediately, but it rarely takes more than a few hours;
- low cost – a few seconds of phone time and some economic on-line charges;
- received messages can be saved as a file on your disk;
- multiple copies can be sent easily;
- messages can be returned to the sender or forwarded on to other people, after editing and annotating.

One of the disadvantages of e-mail is that it will not arrive if there is the slightest error in the address – there is no human postman to work out what you meant.

A second disadvantage is that, unlike the post, which is delivered to the door, e-mail has to be collected. Not everyone does this as regularly as you might hope, so even though your message may be delivered almost immediately, it may not be read for some time.

E-mail can be more de-humanized and impersonal than using conventional post. With sensitivity, however, this does not have to be the case.

E-mail addresses

Before you can write to anyone, you must know their address. Now, while addresses follow simple rules and are fairly easy to remember, you cannot work them out for yourself and you must get them exactly right. The basic pattern is:

name@site.address

Notice the punctuation – an @ sign after the name, and dots between the constituent parts of the site address.

The **name** is usually based on the user's real name, though with lots if variations. Spaces are either ignored or replaced by – (underscore) or . (full stop). Sometimes a number will be added, especially to common names. Some organizations ignore the person's real name completely and allocate numbers or special user names. 'Johnny B. Goode', for example, might be allocated the names 'jbgoode', 'johnnyg', 'John_Goode', 'johnny.b.goode', 'goode3' or something entirely different.

The **site address** will normally be the name of the service provider or of the business or other organization to which the person belongs. For example, individuals who have BT Internet as their service provider have e-mail addresses that end '@btinternet.com', while addresses of the staff at Hodder and Stoughton end '@hodder.co.uk'.

Knowing the pattern will help you to recognize an e-mail addresses, but it is not enough to enable you to work out a person's address. The simplest way to get someone's address is to ask them. If this is not possible, you may be able to find it through the Internet. CompuServe, AOL and other large Service Providers have directories that members can access to find the addresses of other members, and there are 'people-finding' sites on the World Wide Web that have (incomplete) directories of e-mail addresses.

Using e-mail

On the whole, using e-mail is more like having a conversation than receiving a letter and the immediacy of it can breed a casual sloppinness that can lack identity or originality. The art of letter writing – a reflective and introspective process – can be lost in the speed.

People who work in large offices continually e-mail each other and sometimes hardly ever see their colleagues. This is a pity. While more distilled than a real conversation, by its very brevity e-mail would not convey an attitude or an inflection.

Whilst e-mail more efficiently replaces the office memo, letter-writing skills are still essential to use it effectively. The following example is too casual and does not include sufficient information:

> Hi Jake
> Let me have an opinion on the Madison Account. You remember we talked about it last week. They don't seem to be handling their end that well. Can you react ASAP.

This has the vaguest possible detail and doesn't give the recipient any chance to produce a reasoned and informed reply. They will now have to recall the conversation of last week, as well as having to research the reason why Madison aren't handling their 'end' that well. Although brevity is important when using e-mail, try to ensure that your message is sufficiently factual:

> Jake,
> I'm worried about the Madison Account. They haven't reacted to our latest set of figures, neither have they provided the right copy. They seem to be losing interest. Is there anything wrong our end that I don't know about? Let me know what you think.

In order to use e-mail for a proper letter you should follow the same rules as have been previously discussed in this book, but the main advantage is immediacy. You can update or change details very quickly as the following examples underline:

Dear Sue
I've looked forward so much to our holiday and am sending you a few prices for our possible Greek Island wandering. If, on the other hand, you still hanker for Israel, I've included some details of the resorts on the Dead Sea. I'm just checking on the prices and will send them through in an hour or so.
Much love
Tom

Then, an hour later, not only come the prices but also another idea:

Dear Sue
The price for the Dead Sea hotels range from ... to ... but I've also had another idea. What about riding through the Cervennes? After all, we're both experienced with horses and you know how much we enjoyed Ireland. I've contacted the stables in France on their own e-mail and they've sent me the prices which I think you'll agree are amazingly cheap.
Let me know what you think by this afternoon.
Much love
Tom

When Sue wants to reply to Tom's e-mail, she can include his message in her reply. This saves typing, but more importantly shows that she is responding to his ideas point by point. The e-mail software will have identified the included text (normally by > at the start of each line) so that it is easily distinguished from the new text of the reply.

Dear Tom

>The price for the Dead Sea hotels range from
>... to ... but I've also had another idea.
as long as we aim for the lower end of the range!
>What about riding through the Cervennes? After
How far? How many hours in the saddle?

>know how much we enjoyed Ireland. I've contact
yes, but the riding was very easy and those country pub lunches really made it
>they've sent me the prices which I think you'll
>agree are amazingly cheap.

Let me have them!

Thanks for chasing round on this. See you later.

Sue

You will notice that Sue has edited the original message, leaving only those lines to which she wants to respond. This is good practice. There is no point in sending lines that you are not commenting on, and it takes only a moment to edit a message down to the essentials.

Copies and mailing lists

At the simplest, a message is sent to one person, but e-mail offers very efficient ways to communicate to any number of people at once.

Most e-mail software can handle three categories of recipients:

- **To:** the main recipient(s).
- **CC:** (Carbon Copies) people to whom you want to send copies, and whose names you want to appear on the message.
- **BCC:** (Blind Carbon Copies) people who will receive copies, but whose names will not appear on the message.

You can include any number of people in any of the categories when sending a message. As a general rule, use To: for those people from whom you expect a reply; use CC: for those who you just want to keep informed of what's happening. BCC: is rarely used, as you would normally let your recipients know who else would be reading the message. A key exception would be in mailing lists (see below), where the names of others on the list would be irrelevant to other members.

Where e-mails are regularly copied to the same group of people, for example, members of a project team, their addresses can be formed into a group address. Selecting the group as the recipient in your e-mail software would then cause copies to be sent to all members of the group.

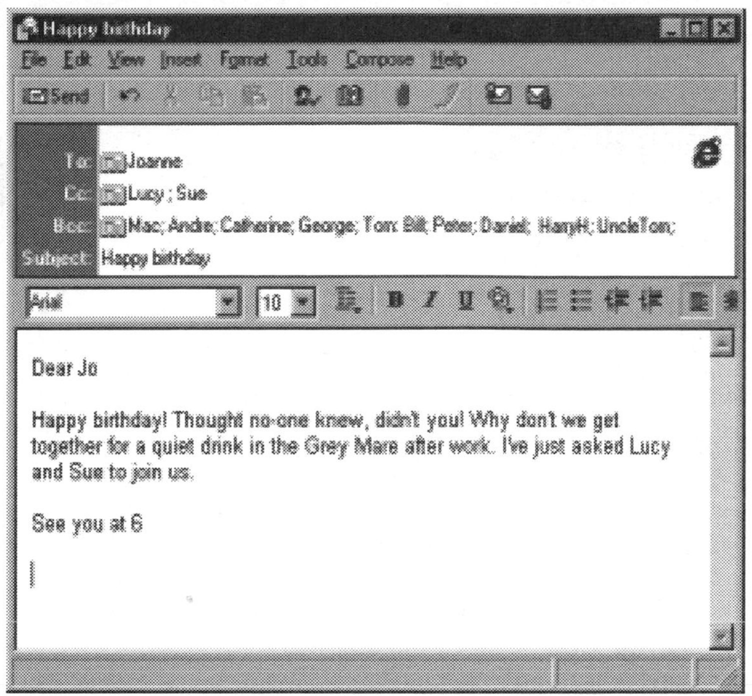

Figure caption: Multiple copies of the same message can be sent to different categories of recipient at the same time. Note the Subject line in the top pane. Its purpose is to enable your recipients to organize their incoming mail.

Mailing lists are a development of this idea. They are used for circulating newsletters to hundreds or thousands of people at a time through the Internet.

Word processors and e-mail editors

The quickest way to write an e-mail message is to use the mail system's own editor. Unfortunately, these rarely include a spell-checker, though they are beginning to appear on newer systems.

If you are a poor typist or an indifferent speller, you would be advized to write the message in your normal wordprocessor – and spell-check it! It can then be copied from there to the mail editor, using the computer's Cut and Paste facility, or sent as a file attached to a brief covering message.

You will be surprised at the number of typing errors that you find in people's e-mail. Don't add to the number if you can help it.

Incoming mail

When you collect your mail, it will normally be placed into an 'In-box', where it will appear as a single line entry showing the sender, the date and whatever the sender wrote in their Subject line. After looking at the sender and the subject, you can decide whether you want to read it immediately, later or not at all. (There is a certain amount of junk mail that can find its way into your box.) If you store messages for long-term reference, those subject lines will help to identify them.

Double-clicking on a message will open it in a viewing window, where you can read it. Any good e-mail software will give you several options for dealing with mail. You should be able to:

- **reply**, including the original text, if desired. You can edit that text, to cut out unwanted material and add comments
- **forward** the mail to someone else, perhaps after editing
- **save** the message as a plain text file
- **copy or cut** part of the message, pasting it into a word-processed file, using the standard Windows Edit routines
- **delete** the message.

methods of address

In this chapter you will learn:

- **about the correct way to address somebody in a letter**
- **specifically about how to address those with ecclesiastical titles, medics and those with academic degrees**
- **how to address prime ministers, presidents, ambassadors, mayors and other officials**
- **the correct way to address an envelope.**

When the final draft of a letter has been completed, two more decisions must be taken.

1 Style of address: the opening words of the letter, i.e. 'Dear ... (whoever you are writing to)'
2 The superscription: the form in which the name of your correspondent will appear on the envelope, for example 'The Right Honourable Sir John Smith, PC, DSO, MP'.

In some cases there are definite rules, but there are others where the writer can use discretion. In doing this he or she should take into account the known views of the correspondent, the degree of acquaintance, and the relative status of the person addressed.

Style of address

Nowadays, the use of 'Dear Sir/Madam', concluding 'Yours faithfully', is only used when writing to a large corporation. Where possible you should find out the name of the appropriate person and write 'Dear Ms Edwards' or 'Dear Mr Mason', concluding 'Yours sincerely'. In the absence of a specific name, the title of the job would do, e.g. 'Dear Customer Relations', again concluding 'Yours sincerely'. In this way you can avoid being labelled sexist.

A doctor who has no other title is simply addressed as 'Dear Dr Smith' unless he or she is either a surgeon or a doctor of medicine who has attained consultant status, in which case the correct form of address is 'Mr or Ms Smith'.

A professor (even if also a Doctor) is addressed as 'Dear Professor Smith'.

If the doctor or professor has any other title (e.g. peerage, Service or ecclesiastical rank, or one derived from a high appointment), this technically takes precedence. Therefore, when Dr Smith becomes a Canon he should be addressed as 'Canon Smith'; when Professor John Smith becomes a knight, he should be addressed as 'Dear Sir John'. If Canon Smith inherits a peerage title, or Sir John has one conferred upon him, then in both cases they would become 'Dear Lord Smith'.

While this is the correct procedure, there are one or two holders of multiple titles who prefer to be known by the title they value most, i.e. a professorship rather than some inherited title. If you know this to be the case it is courteous to respect personal preference.

Ecclesiastical titles

In addressing those with ecclesiastical titles below the rank of Bishop, the forms 'Dear Rev Sir' or 'Very Rev Sir' (for a Dean) or 'Venerable Sir' (for an Archdeacon) are little used today. It is better to say 'Dear Mr Blank', or in the case of a Roman Catholic priest or Anglican who elects to use this title, 'Dear Father Blank'. Similarly for holders of doctorates or those of higher ecclesiastical rank, 'Dear Doctor (or Canon or Archdeacon or Monsignor) Blank'.

The old fulsome preambles for bishops and higher ranks are no longer used except in formal ecclesiastical documents. The modern forms of address, formal and less formal respectively, are:

Bishop:	'My Lord', 'My Lord Bishop', or 'Dear Bishop Blank' (using his surname, not the name of his see)
Archbishop:	'My Lord Archbishop' (or more usually nowadays, 'Your Grace'), or 'Dear Archbishop Blank'
Cardinal:	'My Lord Cardinal', or 'Dear Cardinal Blank'

Titles derived from appointments

There is no special form of address for the Prime Minister. The form 'Dear Prime Minister' is not used in business correspondence but only in letters from colleagues or friends. The President of the United States would be addressed as 'Mr President'.

Ambassadors are addressed as 'Your Excellency' (formal), or 'Dear Mr Smith' or 'Dear Lord Exton'.

The title Lord Mayor is restricted to the chief official of some large towns, including: London, Birmingham, Liverpool, Manchester, Sheffield, Leeds, Bristol, Hull, Newcastle-upon-Tyne, Nottingham, Bradford, York, Coventry, Norwich, Plymouth, Portsmouth, Stoke-on-Trent, Cardiff, Belfast,

Dublin, Cork and certain cities within the Commonwealth. In Scotland the equivalent title is Lord Provost – for Edinburgh, Aberdeen, Dundee and Glasgow. The Scottish equivalent of Mayor is Provost.

Certain officials are entitled to be styled 'Right Honourable' (usually abbreviated to 'Rt Hon') even when not addressed by name. These include:

'The Rt Hon the Lord Advocate'
'The Rt Hon the Lord High Chancellor'
'The Rt Hon the Lord Chief Justice of England'

A Privy Councillor is entitled to the same prefix, with the letters 'PC' following his name, e.g.:

'The Rt Hon John Smith, PC'

A Lord Mayor of London, York, Belfast, Dublin, Cork and of certain Commonwealth capitals (including Sydney, Melbourne, Adelaide, Perth, Brisbane and Hobart) is also addressed as:

'The Rt Hon the Lord Mayor of ...'

The chief officials of Edinburgh and Glasgow are similarly:

'The Rt Hon the Lord Provost of ...'

Other Lord Mayors or Lord Provosts are addressed as:

'The Lord Mayor of ...' or 'The Lord Provost of ...'

Mayors of cities are:

'The Right Worshipful Mayor of ...'

Mayors of Boroughs are:

'The Worshipful Mayor of ...'

An Alderman is addressed as 'Mr Alderman Smith'; or, if titled, 'Alderman Sir John Smith', etc.

Superscriptions

The superscription is the name and address as you put it on the envelope.

Doctors, of any faculty and either sex, are addressed as 'Doctor', with the exception of surgeons and medical men and women of consultant status who are addressed as 'Mr, Mrs or Ms'. In the case of those normally addressed (in conversation) as 'doctor', the superscription 'Doctor John Smith', previously regarded as too informal for business use, is now generally accepted.

A professor who is also a doctor is given the superscription 'Professor John Smith'.

Each of the five Lord Justices of Appeal is addressed formally as 'My Lord', the envelope addressed to any such judge should be headed 'The Rt Hon The Lord Justice [Jones]' and on judicial matters he will be addressed as 'His Lordship'.

Judges of the High Court are also addressed on judicial matters as 'My Lord', 'Your Lordship' or 'Your Ladyship', while the envelope should be addressed to: 'The Hon Mr Justice [Jones]' or 'The Hon Mrs Justice [Jones]'.

A County Court Judge should be addressed at the start of a letter as 'Sir' or 'Madam' and the envelope should be addressed to 'His' or 'Her' Honour Judge [Jones]'.

A Justice of the Peace, although addressed as 'Your Worship' when on the Bench, is addressed on an envelope merely as 'Mr John Smith' or 'Ms Mary Smith', followed by 'JP'.

The superscription for an Ambassador should include both rank and name, the diplomatic rank standing before all others, including royal titles, e.g:

> 'His Excellency (Admiral Sir) John Smith, HBM Ambassador to ...'
>
> or:
>
> 'His Excellency Prince' (or Count or whatever the title may be) followed by the name.

The wife of an ambassador is usually given the courtesy title of 'Her Excellency' in the country to which her husband is accredited, although not in her own country. Similarly it is customary to address as 'Her Excellency' the wife of an ambassador accredited to the Court of St James's.

Heads of diplomatic missions which have not been raised to the status of an embassy are not entitled to the rank of Excellency and are addressed by their normal style as 'Mr John Smith' or 'Ms Mary Smith', followed by (in the case of a British Minister) HBM Minister Plenipotentiary to ...'

Consuls of all ranks are similarly addressed as: 'Mr John Smith' or 'Ms Mary Smith', HBM Consul in ...'

The form 'HBM' instead of the more familiar 'HM' is used because in other countries the words 'His or Her Majesty' would not necessarily refer to the British monarch.

While most clergy today welcome, as a sign of their better relationship with the laity, the disuse of the old highly ceremonial forms of address, the correct superscriptions should still be used.

For Anglican clergy the forms are:

'The Rev John Smith'

The word 'Reverend' precedes any temporal title, e.g:

'The Rev Lord John Smith'

'The Rev Hon John Smith' (not 'The Rev and Hon')

The Christian name, or initials, should always be included. If this is not known and cannot be ascertained, a blank must be left, e.g:

'The Rev - Smith'.

A canon or prebendary is addressed in the same way except that this title takes the place of the Christian name or initial:

'The Rev Canon Smith'

'The Rev Prebendary Smith'

The superscription for a Dean is:

'The Very Rev Dean of Exton';

for an Archdeacon:

'The Venerable the Archdeacon of Exton' or 'The Venerable John Smith';

and for a Bishop:

'The Right Rev the Lord Bishop of Exton'.

This is also correct for Suffragan bishops.

A retired bishop is addressed as:

'The Right Rev Bishop Smith'.

The superscription for an Archbishop is:

'His Grace the Lord Archbishop of Exton' or, if retired: 'The Most Rev Archbishop Smith'.

For Roman Catholic clergy the forms are:

Cardinal: 'His Eminence Cardinal John Smith' or, if also an Archbishop, 'His Eminence Cardinal John Smith, Archbishop of Exton' or 'His Eminence the Cardinal Archbishop of Exton'.
Archbishop: 'The Most Rev Archbishop of Exton'.

Bishop: 'The Rt Rev the Bishop of Exton'.

Monsignor: According to rank either 'The Right Rev Mgr John Smith (higher) or 'The Very Rev Mgr John Smith' (lower).

Canon: 'The Very Rev Canon Smith'; or, if also a Monsignor, 'The Right Rev (or Very Rev) Mgr Canon Smith'.

For priests (secular): 'The Rev John Smith'.

Those in religious orders have the initials of their order after their name: 'Rev John Smith, SJ', or 'Rev John Smith OP'.

The Moderator of the Church of Scotland is addressed as 'The Right Rev John Smith' while in office and 'The Very Rev John Smith' when he has relinquished office.

Honours and awards

The superscription should include all honours, awards, academic and other distinctions to which the person is entitled. When addressing anyone who has had a very distinguished career, the simplest way of ensuring that all the letters after his name are included, and in the right order, is to check with an up-to-date book of reference. This, obviously, may not include recent awards.

Academic degrees are given in rising order of importance, that is, Bachelor, Master, Doctor; e.g. BA, BSc, etc; MA, MMs, etc; DPhil, DSc, etc. But only the highest distinction gained in any one faculty is normally used.

Although it is not correct to include academic distinctions below the grade of doctor (such as BSc or MA) in the superscription of private letters, these are usually included for the purposes of business correspondence, if their existence is known to the writer.

Academic degrees are followed by professional qualifications, and abbreviations denoting 'Fellows', 'Licentiates' and 'Members' of professional bodies. As far as these last are concerned, there is no order of preference sufficiently generally used by their holders to be regarded as even customary.

Some people opt for descending order of importance as with 'honours', others choose rising order and put fellowships last; some place distinctions awarded by senior bodies before those awarded by newer bodies; others follow the order in which the distinctions were obtained, simply adding on any additional qualifications as these come along, e.g. 'MRCS, LRCP (Member of the Royal College of Surgeons, and Licentiate of the Royal College of Physicians) or 'LRCP, MRCS'. Whatever the order, only the highest grade of membership of any professional body is included, e.g. 'MRCS' is discarded once the holder becomes an 'FRCS'.

'JP' (Justice of the Peace) follows such professional qualifications, immediately preceding 'MP'.

index